¡Ceviche!

¡Ceviche!

SEAFOOD, SALADS, AND COCKTAILS WITH A LATINO TWIST

by Guillermo Pernot with Aliza Green | Foreword by John Mariani

RUNNING PRESS
PHILADELPHIA · LONDON

9   8   7   6   5   4   3   2   1
Digit on the right indicates the number of this printing

Library of Congress Cataloging-in-Publication Number 2001087066

ISBN 0-7624-1043-4

Cover and interior photography: Steve Legato
Cover and interior designer: Alicia Freile
Editor: Janet Bukovinsky Teacher
Project Editor: Melissa Wagner
Typography: Univers, Sabon, and New Berolina

This book may be ordered by mail from the publisher.
Please include $2.50 for postage and handling.
But try your bookstore first!

Running Press Book Publishers
125 South Twenty-second Street
Philadelphia, Pennsylvania 19103-4399

Visit us on the web!
www.runningpress.com

Acknowledgments

There are many friends, employees, employers, and family members who have been instrumental in my growth as a chef over the past ten years. I would never be where I am today without the loving support and encouragement of my wife, Lucia. She helped me follow my dreams and, with my mother-in-law, Totty (a superb cook), taught me about the wonderful food of their native Cuba. David Scharro opened a small Italian restaurant and gave me my first opportunity to put my creativity to the test. As a restaurateur, he gave a young chef a great start, but in his second career as a general contractor, David can be credited with building ¡Pasión! with all the skill and care I could have wished for.

Several people supported me while I continued to grow as a chef. My partner, Michael Dombkoski, and his family were there as guinea pigs from the beginning. They came to eat wherever I cooked, never imagining that our individual dreams of owning a restaurant would someday come true in the form of ¡Pasión!. Michael's commitment to great service and his ability to train knowledgeable servers allows me to concentrate on what I do best. Without him, neither ¡Pasión! nor this cookbook would be a reality.

The other anchor that keeps ¡Pasión! grounded is my chef de cuisine, Michael McMillan. He has been with me for five years now. We have grown together and continue to feed off each other's creativity. I'm honored to work with such a talented chef at my side. The rest of my staff, from those in the prep kitchen to the hot line cooks and the skilled servers, is equally important. I could not do what I do without them, for they are truly committed. In fact, they are the passion behind ¡Pasion!.

I would be remiss if I did not mention Elaine Tait and Aliza Green. Through their very generous attention in their columns and reviews, both of these writers helped introduce my food to places it may have never reached. They understood my food and saw it for what it was five years ago—the future of the culinary world. They were instrumental in helping me introduce my food to the Philadelphia area and well beyond.

Sammy D'Angelo of Samuel & Son Seafood Company and Hesh of Hesh's Seafood both provided me with pristine seafood on demand, while Anthropologie generously lent me some of the eclectic tableware for these beautiful photos.

Without Aliza Green and Stephen Legato, this book would not have been possible. I want to thank Stephen for taking on the challenge of photographing ceviche and making it look as beautiful as it is delicious, while constantly maintaining his calm sense of humor. Aliza's insight into my cooking, and the long summer days spent in my kitchen with me, making every ceviche and trying each recipe, was truly a labor of love.

Foreword

A dozen or so years ago at a symposium on Pan-American food, a very well-traveled speaker asked the audience, "Seriously now, folks, has any of you ever really had a good meal anywhere in the Caribbean?" The laughter and wagging heads in the audience indicated that few ever had, and no one else on the seminar panel could disagree. Nor could I.

Things have improved a great deal in the Caribbean and Latin American countries since then, although the commitment to a truly modern Pan-Am cuisine took root in the United States long before it did down there. Led by young chefs in Miami—most of them non-Latinos like Mark Militello, Pascal Oudin, Alan Susser, and Norman van Aken—this new "Floribbean" cuisine had bite, color, and local flavors based on the freshest seasonal ingredients. That much of it went too far in a direction that bore little resemblance to the true cooking of these regions was evident in splashy plate displays and mismatched ingredients, often with too many fiery chile peppers that obliterated the other ingredients.

All such culinary movements need time to cure and simmer, and it was not until the 1998 opening of ¡Pasion!—in, of all places, Philadelphia—that I was convinced the movement had depth, ballast, and a real leader. He is Guillermo Pernot, an Argentinean by birth who does indeed show passion for creating a modern Pan-American cuisine that wholly respects traditions within the diverse food cultures of Central America, South America, and the Caribbean. He applies more focus, understanding, and intelligence to the ingredients than do many of his peers, some of whom seem to think up a dish on the spur of the evening.

More than any other chef working within the Pan-Am (now called "Nuevo Latino") medium today, Pernot proves that such well-seasoned cookery can be appreciated for its refinement, rather than simply for the heat of its chile peppers, or the salsa music playing in the dining room.

His finesse with exotic ingredients like cancha, yuca, annatto, and calabaza is amazing; his marinated ceviches have a clarity of taste others' lacked; and his ability to convince sometimes squeamish Americans to taste and then love octopus, monkfish liver, and curried king mackerel has made him a crusader. Pernot's predilection for fried boniato, rice croquetas, tostones de platano, and similar down-home, regional items has been just what the movement needs to prove it has substance, not just razzle-dazzle.

In his new book, Guillermo masterfully demonstrates how such delectable dishes can be made at home, giving precise details on handling fish correctly, using exotic fruits and vegetables, and making food so beautiful that your guests will revel in its symmetry of color, aroma, and style.

Were anyone to ask the question posed earlier—"Has anyone really ever had a good meal in the Caribbean?"—I could reel off a score of places where I have indeed dined well in recent years. But if I wanted you to experience the very best of Nuevo Latino food in its brightest, most savory form, I'd still send you to Philly, to a place with a name that tells you everything you need to know about the food, and about the man who created it.

—John Mariani
January 2001

Introductory Note

I met Guillermo Pernot about twenty years ago, when I was chef at Ristorante DiLullo in Philadelphia and he worked the front of the house. Later, I moved to another renowned restaurant, Apropos, where Guillermo turned up again. While I had children, worked as a consultant, and began to write, Guillermo made the long leap to the back of the house and became an acclaimed chef.

After opening his own restaurant, ¡Pasion!, and establishing its reputation as one of the top Latino eateries in this country, Guillermo was ready to share his recipes. When he approached me about co-authoring his ceviche cookbook, I was excited. I wanted to learn a new culinary vocabulary by helping to prepare, style, and translate his recipes into cookbook form.

We were lucky enough to work with the talented photographer Steve Legato. For several months, we all came to the kitchen of ¡Pasión! early each day to set up the photo shoots while making notes about the ceviches that Guillermo had created. The ¡Pasión! staff, who often had to work around us, was invariably gracious. I got to meet a kitchen full of professionals, many of them Hispanic, who shone with pride in their skills.

During that time, I had the chance to work with all sorts of new fish and seafood varieties. Guillermo taught me how to cut fish for ceviche, and shared other tips and tricks, many of them from his mother. I learned to identify new pantry items and seasonings from Peru, Brazil, Argentina, Cuba, and elsewhere in Latin America. I've been lucky enough to explore such regional ingredients as yuca, cilantro, and mango on my own, through my weekly column for the *Philadelphia Inquirer*. Having had the pleasure of working with Guillermo and tasting his food, my own cooking has been enriched and has become much more piquant.

—Aliza Green

Introduction

I am a fanatical aficionado of ceviche. These marinated fish and seafood dishes are native to Peru and parts of Chile, Ecuador, and Honduras, and are popular elsewhere in Latin America, including Mexico's Pacific coast, the Yucatan, and the Caribbean. In Argentina, where I grew up, ceviche was never on the menu. I first tasted it when I was sixteen. En route from Los Angeles, where I had been visiting relatives, to Buenos Aires, I was bumped from a flight in Lima, Peru. I ended up spending four days on my own, reveling in the discovery of delicious ceviches made from shrimp, lobster, and black clams.

Later, when I was already in the food business, I went on vacation to the lovely and somewhat inaccessible Isla Mujeres off the southern coast of Yucatan, near Cancun. Maybe it's because I was so relaxed, but the ceviches I tasted at the snorkeling paradise of El Garafon on Mujeres were absolutely wonderful. They were made from the native sea turtle, red snapper, and conch in a simple fresh lime marinade. Then and there I learned that the best ceviche is made from the freshest and usually the most common ingredients.

My enthusiasm was heightened when I began enjoying and being fascinated by sushi. I loved the impeccably fresh seafood and fish sushi that I ate at New York's Nobu, made by legendary chef Nobu Matsuhishu. His dishes gave me a benchmark by which to judge the ceviches I would eventually create. From him I learned to use only the finest quality (and very expensive) sushi-grade fish and seafood, and to marinate the product very lightly, rather than curing it for days in the classic Peruvian style. Now I think it's funny that Japanese sushi chefs like Nobu, and Taka [Eji Takase] of Sushi Samba in New York, have started to bring Latin American flavors into their sushi. At the same time, I have been incorporating both sushi standards of quality and Asian flavors into my ceviche.

In 1996, when I was finally in charge of my own kitchen at Vega Grill in Philadelphia, I was inspired by the ground-breaking cooking of the Nuevo Latino chef Douglas Rodriguez. At his restaurant Patria, I was impressed by his imaginative ceviches. I remember one made with squid in a black ink sauce; a spicy shrimp ceviche with popcorn he adapted from an Ecuadorean recipe. Until I ate Rodriguez's ceviche, I had enjoyed the dish but was a little bored by it. As a chef, I'd felt that the flavors were too predictable and limited. Douglas helped me see my way out of the box.

All of a sudden I understood the limitless possibilities of the dish, and I started experimenting. I was determined to combine the outstanding quality of the best sushi with the bold flavors of Latin American ceviche. At first, I was rather nervous because I wasn't sure my customers would accept these new creations. I decided to trust in my culinary roots, and started to present dishes with yuca, platanos, boniato, culantro, and other ingredients. Back then, I actually had to teach many of my purveyors about these Latino products and where to get them.

I served my first ceviche at Vega Grill. It was Chilean sea bass, Japanese seaweed salad, and purée of sweet, starchy boniato, all layered in a martini glass. The dish really took off, and I was soon buying hundreds of pounds of Chilean sea bass a week to keep up with the demand.

Once I had the opportunity to open my own restaurant, ¡Pasión!, I knew that I wanted to feature ceviche. I had all sorts of ideas. Originally, I planned to build a special ceviche bar with seats facing the ceviche chef, similar to the sushi bars of Japanese restaurants. I wanted to serve my ceviche in frozen bamboo stalks held in a special metal caddy, but had to give up on that idea when I found that large enough bamboo was almost impossible to come by.

Then I was going to serve it in abalone shells (and in this book, I do present my abalone ceviche in beautiful natural shells). I finally ended up building a dedicated ceviche station inside the kitchen and serving my ceviche in special glass dishes from Venezuela nestled into a bed of crushed ice sprinkled with colorful bits of chiles and cilantro. You could, of course, borrow my ideas and serve your ceviche in bamboo or natural shells.

The challenge of serving ceviche in a restaurant is that each dish has to be made individually, by assembling the components, seasoning them, and arranging them attractively for serving. I am eternally grateful to my kitchen staff because every day and with every ceviche, they make me look good. They've also helped me by coming up with good ideas to incorporate into future ceviche creations. As a home cook, you have the advantage in being able to prepare and season your ceviche until it tastes just right to you.

Almost all the ceviches in this book are relatively simple, though some include different components that must be prepared separately. The simplest is my perennially popular Bay Scallop Ceviche with Blackened Tomatillo–Truffle Sauce. I can assure you that it's not too difficult because I recently prepared 11,000 (yes, really!) portions, all served on spoons, as a guest chef at the Toronto Film Festival. Other good choices for beginners are Red Snapper Ceviche with Avocado Mash, Tobiko Wasabi Vinaigrette and Peppercress Salad, and Big-Eye Tuna Ceviche Picadillo with Maduros.

I recommend serving ceviche as an appetizer or a light lunch dish, especially in hot weather. However, you can certainly serve it whenever you get the best quality ingredients. My customers don't seem to care how cold it is outside! Ninety percent of them order ceviche because I've become so well known for it. At home, you might want to make ceviche for a small group. Eight guests or fewer is preferable, because it's a little harder to control when you're making large quantities. Remember to chill your plates, and make sure that the ceviche itself is icy cold.

For anyone concerned about the food safety issues, I have consulted many sources and come up with a list of recommendations for making as sure as possible that your ceviche is safe to eat. Keep in mind, however, that there is always a very small risk involved, although it's no greater than if you eat raw milk cheeses, prepared food from a take-out store, or medium-rare fish or meat in a restaurant.

All chefs love to eat; I am no exception. Eating has always been a passion for me. Perhaps a bigger passion has been for the process and ceremony involved in cooking. As a child growing up in Argentina, I spent many hours with my mother and grandmother in the kitchen. Their traditions of meal preparation and the ways in which food affected our lives remain with me. We never cooked a meal quickly before rushing off somewhere else. We gave food the attention and respect it deserves. Every day at ¡Pasión! I try to treat my food with the same degree of respect and love because I know that for my customers, a meal at ¡Pasión! must be an experience to recall with pleasure.

I never attended culinary school or had the opportunity to train under world-renowned chefs, but I also know that neither guarantees talent, great food, or success in your own restaurant. I've always followed my instincts because I believe that having the strength in your own gut and the love for what you do is the key to succeeding in the vast, frenzied, and competitive food business.

I have been very lucky with my staff. They've been loyal and supportive, perhaps because they know how hard I've had to work to establish my own reputation. Over the years, I have hired many untrained cooks. Though they may be just starting out in the restaurant business, everyone who works in my kitchen must have a passion for cooking and for learning. I continue to learn much from them.

My ceviche creations have become a signature at ¡Pasión!. People talk about them, and customers can't seem get enough of them. I wanted to share my recipes, so I got together with two great collaborators, writer Aliza Green and photographer Steve Legato, and we set to work. I hope that after trying my recipes, you will be just as crazy about these light, flavorful, and ultra-fresh dishes as I am.

—Guillermo Pernot

Chef's Techniques

To Slice Fish

Start with three essentials: a well-scrubbed cutting board, sanitized with a mixture of 1 tablespoon bleach in 1 quart water; a very sharp knife with a 10-inch blade; and fresh, very cold fish. Before cutting, wrap the fish fillets in plastic wrap and place in the freezer for about 30 minutes, or until firm and somewhat stiff. Using a very sharp knife, cut straight across the fillet, starting from the head end and continuing to cut about three-quarters of the way down the fillet. Discard the tail end of the fillet, which is too stringy to use.

To Cut Bell Peppers into Brunoise Dice

To cut peppers very evenly, slice off and discard ½ inch from the tops and bottoms. Cut down the side and open up each pepper, spreading it to flatten. Using a sharp slicing knife, cut parallel to the flesh to remove the white membrane with seeds and a bit of the inside layer of flesh. Cut into ¼-inch strips, and then cut the strips into squares.

To Cut Herbs into Chiffonade

I really dislike finely chopped herbs with the excess liquid squeezed out, in the technique used in French kitchens. I feel that the flavor of the herb diminishes with all the chopping: the more you chop, the more it bruises the leaves, which makes them deteriorate quickly. This makes it necessary to squeeze out and discard the flavorful juices of herbs such as Italian parsley, which is a pity.

Instead, pick the leaves of the herbs and wash them in a large bowl of cold water, swishing around vigorously to encourage any sand to fall to the bottom of the bowl. I use a slotted spoon or wire skimmer to scoop the leaves from the water and place them in a colander to drain, shaking occasionally to get rid of more water. Dry the leaves in a salad spinner and spread them out on paper towels to dry completely.

Grasp a handful of leaves, rolling them up into a compact package. Using a heavy, sharp chopping knife, cut across the leaves in thin slices, rolling the leaves back up to compact them as you chop. You should end up with thin strips of leaves, called chiffonade. To store, place the sliced leaves in a dampened paper towel. Roll up loosely and place in a zipper-lock bag. Note that herbs should be stored in the warmest part of the refrigerator. Many herbs, in particular basil and tarragon, are sensitive to cold and will blacken and begin to spoil if kept too cold.

To Peel Chiles by Deep-Frying

A quick method for peeling chiles is to heat 2 to 3 cups of vegetable oil in a wok until shimmering hot. Drop in 2 or 3 chiles at a time, enough to fit comfortably without crowding. Fry until the skins turn dark brown. Have ready a large bowl of water mixed with ice. Remove the fried chiles from the oil and drop immediately into the cold water to stop the cooking. Rub off the skins, and then open up and remove the seeds before proceeding with your recipe.

To Prepare Tamarind

Tamarind is usually sold dried, in small blocks that weigh about ¾ pound and keep indefinitely. The blocks must be soaked to soften, and the solids strained out to obtain the usable fruit pulp. Cover the block in hot water and soak it for about 30 minutes, or until the tamarind has softened. Break up the pulp with your hands to speed the process. Rub the tamarind with its liquid through a sieve or food mill, discarding the fibers and seeds. The resulting pulp is ready to use and will keep for at least a month in the refrigerator.

How to Make a Hot Smoker

For both hot and cold smoking, you'll need to work outside to ensure good ventilation and avoid setting off the smoke alarm. Home exhaust hoods, unlike their restaurant counterparts, are not powerful enough to eliminate heavy smoke.

First assemble the following components:
- An outdoor barbecue grill with a lid, or heavy-duty foil to cover the grill.
- A bag of wood chips, such as hickory or a fruitwood like cherry or applewood. I don't like to use mesquite chips because the flavor is too strong.
- A deep metal pan (such as a roasting pan) to hold the wood chips. Note that

once you use the pan for smoking, you won't ever be able to use it for anything else.

■ A metal rack to hold the food to be smoked, such as a wire cake cooling rack or a perforated metal grilling pan.

■ 4 well-packed balls of aluminum foil, each about the size of a baseball, to hold the rack.

Fire up the grill, which can be fueled with charcoal or gas, although it's easier to control the temperature with gas. When the grill is evenly heated to a low temperature, you are ready to start smoking.

Cover the bottom of the metal pan with a layer of wood chips about 1 inch deep. Place the 4 foil balls in the corners of the pan atop the chips, and lay the rack on top. Arrange the food you're going to smoke in an even layer on the rack. Place the pan over the fire and heat until the wood chips ignite and start to smoke vigorously. They should continue to burn during the smoking process, forming coals.

Cover the whole assembly tightly with the lid or the foil, and smoke for 6 to 8 minutes, depending on the thickness of the food. Ultimately, you will need to taste it to see if it has absorbed sufficient smoke flavor. Note that in hot smoking, you are both smoking and cooking the food; so it will change texture as it cooks. Also, if the food to be smoked is quite thick, you may wish to smoke it and then finish cooking in a slow oven, at about 250°F, to avoid imparting too strong a smoked flavor.

The smoke should never be thick and white in color, an indication that it is too hot. You should just be able to see thin strands of smoke escaping. Overly hot smoke will result in a bitter taste—one of the most common problems when smoking food.

How to Make a Cold Smoker

If you have a gas stove, you can use the open flame on your stovetop to start the wood chips smoldering, as long as you smother the fire and carry the smoking assembly outside immediately afterward to avoid filling the kitchen with smoke. You can also use an outdoor barbecue grill to ignite the wood chips or, of course, a smoker made just for that purpose.

First assemble the following components:

■ A bag of wood chips, such as hickory or a fruitwood like cherry or apple-wood. I don't like to use mesquite chips because the flavor is too strong.

■ A small metal pan (such as a cake pan) or a large empty can to hold the wood chips. Note that once you use the pan for smoking, you won't ever be able to use it for anything else.

■ A large, damp towel you can throw away.

■ A large container to hold the whole assembly, which could be a large metal stockpot, a metal storage box or file drawer, or even a large cardboard box.

■ 2 metal racks to hold the food to be smoked, such as wire cake cooling racks or perforated metal grilling pans.

■ 4 well-packed balls of aluminum foil, each about the size of a baseball, to hold 1 rack.

■ A large pan full of ice, plus more ice to replace it once it melts.

Cover the bottom of the pan with a layer of wood chips about 1 inch deep. Place the pan over an open flame and heat until the wood chips ignite and start to smoke vigorously. Smother the fire completely by covering the smoker with a damp towel

Remove the towel and place the pan with the chips in the bottom of the large container. Arrange the foil balls in or alongside the pan and cover with the first wire rack. Place the pan filled with the ice atop the rack. Arrange the food to be smoked in an even layer on the second rack and set it over the pan of ice. Your object here is to cool the smoke by passing it over the ice.

Cover the container tightly with a lid or a double thickness of heavy-duty aluminum foil. Smoke for about 30 minutes, depending on the thickness of the food to be smoked. Check after 30 minutes—if the ice is melted, discard the water from the ice bowl, replace with fresh ice, and smoke 30 minutes longer. You will need to taste the food to see if it has absorbed sufficient smoke flavor. Note that in cold smoking, you are not actually cooking the food, just flavoring it. It should maintain its uncooked texture.

Quick Tips for Seafood Safety

Eating ceviche is one of life's pleasures, but safe preparation practices are essential. Every day around the world people enjoy raw seafood in many forms: ceviche (fish and seafood marinated in lime juice); lomi-lomi (salmon marinated in lemon juice, onions, and tomatoes); *poisson cru* (fish marinated in citrus juice, onions, tomatoes, and coconut milk); sashimi (chunks of raw fish); sushi (raw fish rolled with rice and other ingredients); green herring (lightly brined); drunken crabs (marinated in wine and peppers); and cold-smoked fish.

Unlike more classic ceviche, which might be cured for up to three days so that the protein is completely opaque, my ceviche is very lightly cured, so that the fish or seafood is just beginning to turn opaque. Be aware that curing in lime juice or other acid juices does not cook the food. It does coagulate the proteins, transforming them visually from clear, when the protein molecules are orderly, to solid-looking, when the protein molecules form a thick web. Curing fish and seafood does help preserve it, but it does *not* kill bacteria or parasites.

Admittedly, eating raw seafood is riskier than eating cooked foods, but with reasonable care and a bit of knowledge, you can minimize the risks. Almost any raw seafood can cause illness, so follow these sensible rules for seafood safety, recommended by the Food and Drug Administration.

For more complete information, see Seafood Safety in Detail on page 188.

■ Purchase only the highest quality, or sushi-grade, seafood for ceviche from a reputable fish and seafood purveyor.

■ Keep seafood extra cold at all times. Ask for a plastic bag filled with crushed ice to help maintain cold temperature on the way home, and get it home quickly.

■ To be extra careful, freeze fish intended to be eaten raw long enough to kill any existing parasites.

■ Keep "live" shellfish alive in the refrigerator with good ventilation and moderately cold temperature.

■ Scrub shellfish well only when you're ready to prepare the ceviche, because washing shellfish in fresh water tends to shorten its life.

■ When handling seafood, avoid cross-contamination by preventing raw seafood juices from dripping or splashing onto other food. Be careful not to transfer bacteria from one area to another.

■ Thaw frozen seafood overnight in the refrigerator, never at room temperature, both to ensure best quality and to prevent bacteria growth. The rule is: Freeze it quickly and thaw it slowly.

■ Always buy clams, oysters, and mussels from a licensed, reputable dealer and avoid "bargains."

■ If your immune system is compromised, avoid eating all raw mollusks and be sure to freeze fish long enough to kill parasites.

■ Never eat dead shellfish. Clams, mussels, and live scallops should have unbroken, tightly closed shells. Lobsters, crayfish, and crabs should move.

■ When cooking seafood, cook to an internal temperature of at least 145°F to ensure safety.

■ Use ice and ice water to cool cooked seafood as rapidly as possible.

■ Be aware that certain fish, such as escolar and Japanese blowfish *(fugu)*, carry naturally occurring toxins. Do not use them. It is especially important to purchase only the highest-quality dark-fleshed fish—such as tuna, mackerel, bluefish, mahi-mahi, and amberjack—because they can produce natural toxins if not handled properly while on board fishing vessels.

■ Before preparing ceviche, inspect and then freeze fish that may carry parasites. Cod, plaice, halibut, rockfish, herring, pollock, sea bass, wild salmon, and flounder are subject to parasites. Farm-raised fish such as salmon do not carry parasites. Fish from the West Coast is more likely to be a problem than is fish from the East Coast.

■ Although they are quite rare, be sensitive to seafood allergies and avoid eating any seafood that causes you to have an allergic reaction.

RAW FISH CEVICHE

Spanish Mackerel Ceviche with Pomelo Sections,
Peruvian Huacatay Mint

There are many varieties of mackerel, a dark-meat fish in the same family as tuna and bonito. I use Spanish mackerel, which has a brownish, rough-textured skin. I charbroil the skin, using the pyromaniac chef's favorite tool: a blowtorch, straight from the hardware store. Several cookware catalogs now sell smaller, less fearsome blowtorches that are ideal for this task. Some gourmet shops carry small jars of Huacatay mint purée, a delicious rainforest product from Peru. Because this mint has such a special flavor, I don't recommend any substitutions.

SERVES 4

HUACATAY MINT SAUCE

2 tablespoons Huacatay mint purée
(see Special Ingredients)
¼ cup fresh lime juice
¼ cup mild olive oil
½ teaspoon finely chopped garlic
1 teaspoon kosher salt
2 tablespoons chiffonade of
fresh mint

■ Combine all the ingredients in a blender and purée. Refrigerate, covered, if not using immediately.

MACKEREL AND POMELO CEVICHE

¾ pound fresh Spanish mackerel
fillet with skin
1 pomelo (or white grapefruit)
½ cup Huacatay Mint Sauce

■ Clean the mackerel by placing it skin-side down on a cutting board. Using a sharp knife, cut down along either side of the dark "blood line" that runs along the center. Remove and discard this dark flesh.

■ Using a blowtorch, charbroil the skin of the mackerel until charred and bubbling. Cover and refrigerate the fish until it is firm; then cut crosswise into ½-inch slices.

■ Using a sharp knife, cut away all the skin and the thin outside layer of membrane enclosing the pomelo sections. Cut out each section of fruit from between the membrane on both sides.

■ Using about one-quarter of the Huacatay Mint Sauce, dip each slice of mackerel into the sauce. Cover and refrigerate the fish for about 30 minutes so that it absorbs the flavor of the sauce. When ready to serve, dip each slice of mackerel into the remaining Huacatay Mint Sauce.

■ On a large serving platter, place one pomelo section alongside one slice of the mackerel with the sauce that clings to it. Leave some space between each pair of pomelo and mackerel slices. Drizzle the platter with any remaining sauce and serve immediately.

Pomelo

Pomelo is the original parent of the modern grapefruit. Also known as Thai grapefruit, it is often available at Asian groceries and produce stands. The fruit is extremely large—sometimes as big as a basketball—and has very thick green skin, which must be cut away before use. The flesh is quite firm and a bit dry. Substitute white grapefruit if you can't find pomelo.

Halibut Cheek Ceviche with Asparagus,
Smoked Corn–Amarillo Vinaigrette

The cheek muscles of certain fish, such as cod and halibut, are considered the most delicate and delicious part. Because this richly textured muscle is not easily available to the home cook, I would certainly substitute thinly sliced, very fresh halibut. For the vinaigrette, I lightly hot-smoke the corn on the stovetop, then combine it with sautéed fresh corn so that the smoky flavor isn't overpowering. The corn is puréed with amarillo chile, a deep golden yellow chile pepper beloved in Chile, which I buy in purée form in small jars.

SERVES 4

½ pound halibut cheeks
(or fresh halibut, skinless)

2 tablespoons fresh lime juice

1 teaspoon kosher salt

½ pound medium to large asparagus,
bottom 2 to 3 inches of tough
stem cut off

½ pound fresh jumbo lump
crabmeat, shells picked out and
discarded

¾ cup Smoked Corn–Amarillo
Vinaigrette (see recipe on
page 154)

¾ cup Crunchy Fried Cancha
(see recipe on page 138)

4 fresh blue crab claws, for garnish

■ Using a sharp slicing knife, cut each halibut cheek lengthwise into 3 thin rounds. If using fresh halibut, slice it very thinly. Combine the lime juice and salt, and rub the mixture over the halibut. Cover and refrigerate 20 minutes to marinate. On each of 4 dinner plates, arrange the halibut cheeks in a circle inside the rims. Cover with plastic wrap and press lightly with your hands to flatten the halibut. Refrigerate until ready to serve, up to 4 hours.

■ Bring a medium pot of heavily salted water to the boil. Add the asparagus and cook 2 to 3 minutes, until bright green and tender but still firm. Drain and rinse under cold water to set the color. Reserve 4 attractive asparagus spears for garnish. Cut the remainder into 1-inch lengths on the diagonal, turning a quarter-turn before the next cut so that the diagonal ends face in different directions rather than being parallel.

■ In a small bowl, lightly toss together the asparagus pieces, crabmeat, and ½ cup of the Smoked Corn–Amarillo Vinaigrette. Divide into 4 portions and form the mixture into a mound in the center of each plate containing the halibut. Drizzle the remaining vinaigrette over the halibut and sprinkle with the Crunchy Fried Cancha. Garnish with the crab claws and the reserved asparagus spears. Serve immediately.

Blanching Green Vegetables

I blanch green vegetables like asparagus or green beans to briefly precook them and at the same time maintain their bright, appetizing color. To blanch, bring a medium to large pot of heavily salted water to the boil, using 1 tablespoon of kosher salt per quart of water. Add the vegetables and cook over high heat for several minutes, stirring occasionally so they cook evenly, until they are brilliant green, with no uncooked whitish areas, and tender but still firm. Drain and shock immediately, either by running under cold water or transferring to a bowl of ice mixed with water. I shock vegetables to quickly bring down the temperature, stop the cooking, and set the color.

Fluke Ceviche with Lichee-Lavender Sauce
and Sevruga Caviar

Fluke is a variety of summer flounder that is quite large. It is delicate in flavor, bright white in color, and very delicious in this ceviche with a sauce that combines unusual flavors. You may be skeptical, but I am confident that when you try this dish, you'll agree that lichee fruit and lavender complement each other perfectly. To round out the flavor, I use sevruga caviar, the small, charcoal gray, salted eggs of the sevruga sturgeon, caught only in the Caspian Sea.

The rule for ceviche is the simpler the dish, the fresher the fish needs to be, so buy only the best-quality fluke for this delicate hors d'oeuvre.

SERVES 4

½ pound center-cut fluke fillet, skinless

½ cup fresh lime juice

1 tablespoon kosher salt

¾ pound fresh lichees

½ teaspoon chopped fresh lavender leaves and flowers

½ small habanero chile, trimmed and seeded

1 ounce sevruga caviar

■ Using a sharp knife, slice the fluke very thinly on the bias. Arrange the slices in a single layer in a nonreactive (stainless-steel or enameled) pan. Combine ¼ cup of the lime juice with 2 teaspoons of the salt and pour over the fluke. Cover and refrigerate for at least 20 minutes but no longer than 1 hour. The fresher the fish, the less time it needs to cure. If the raw fish is at all opaque, cure for the full hour.

■ Reserving several whole, unpeeled lichees for garnish, use your thumb to separate the hard, pink skin from the soft flesh of the remaining fruit. Remove and discard all the skin; then pull the lichees open to expose the large pit. Discard the pit and cut the fruit into quarters.

■ Place the remaining ¼ cup lime juice, the remaining teaspoon salt, half the peeled lichee sections, ¼ teaspoon lavender, and habanero in the container of a blender. Purée until smooth and reserve, covered and refrigerated if not using immediately. The sauce keeps well for 3 to 4 days.

■ To serve the ceviche, drain the fluke and arrange it in an attractive pattern on 4 large individual plates. Sprinkle with the remaining ¼ teaspoon of the lavender. Toss the remaining lichee sections with about 2 tablespoons of the sauce. Drizzle the fish with the remaining sauce and place a small mound of lichee sections on each plate.

■ Using a nonmetallic spoon, place a small mound of caviar on each slice of fish. Garnish each plate with 1 or 2 fresh lichees, removing the top portion of the skin to expose the fruit inside if desired. Serve immediately.

Lichees

Lichee is an unusual-looking Asian fruit. Small, pink, and rough-skinned, it is in season in summer and early fall. This delicacy is a taste of paradise, with sweet, juicy, slightly crunchy flesh, lightly but memorably perfumed. While you can substitute the canned lichee fruit sold in Asian markets, it really loses its delicate floral quality in the can and ends up tasting merely sugary-sweet. To prepare fresh lichees, use your fingers to pull off the leathery outer skin. Pull the soft, creamy white flesh away from the dark brown pit.

Hamachi Ceviche with Trio of Peppers Salad,
Citrus Dressing

Hamachi is a rich, flavorful fish in the large tuna-bonito family that comes from Hawaii. It is normally on the expensive side, so I take care to trim the fish very well and use every bit of flesh, especially the wonderful, firm meat near the collarbone. An average hamachi is about twelve pounds, but I'm usually able to buy a single side, shipped from Hawaii in a well-designed, sealed package. I'm particular about cutting the peppers in this dish very thinly, using a mandoline or Benriner cutter. I also trim away a fibrous, watery layer from the inside of the pepper, in order to use only the best-looking, most intensely flavored part. The citrus dressing is also delicious when drizzled over a salad of mixed greens.

SERVES 6

CITRUS DRESSING
½ cup fresh lemon juice
½ cup fresh lime juice
½ cup fresh orange juice
1 tablespoon sugar
2 tablespoons Slow-Roasted Garlic
    Oil (see recipe on page 185)
2 tablespoons Annatto Oil
    (see recipe on page 185)
2 teaspoons kosher salt

■ Combine all the ingredients in the jar of a blender, or use a bowl or jar with an immersion blender. Blend until emulsified and creamy. Reserve at room temperature.

ASSEMBLING THE
HAMACHI CEVICHE
¾ pound skinless hamachi fillet,
    thinly sliced
1 large, evenly shaped red bell pepper
1 large, evenly shaped yellow
    bell pepper
1 large poblano chile

1 cup arugula sprouts, trimmed
    to 2-inch lengths (or 1 cup thinly
    sliced arugula)
½ red onion, sliced very thin and
    rinsed under cold water
Kosher salt and freshly ground
    black pepper

■ In a nonreactive (stainless-steel or enamel) dish, combine the sliced fish with half the Citrus Dressing. Cover and refrigerate for 30 minutes to marinate.

■ Slice ½ inch from the top and bottom of each bell pepper, and discard or reserve the trimmings for another use. Cut along one side of both the bell peppers and the poblano chile, and open up so that each lies flat. Pull out and discard any seeds and white membrane. Using a sharp slicing knife, cut through each pepper parallel to its flat side, to remove the watery-tasting top layer of flesh. The remaining pepper should be rectangular in shape and very thin (less than ⅛-inch thick). Using a mandoline or Benriner cutter, slice each pepper lengthwise into very thin strips, no thicker than thin matchsticks or toothpicks.

■ Toss the peppers with the remaining Citrus Dressing. Lightly toss the fish, pepper mixture, sprouts, and red onion. Adjust the seasoning, adding salt and freshly ground pepper if necessary. Using your fingertips, lightly pinch a mound of the mixture and arrange in a haystack shape on each of 6 chilled salad plates. Serve immediately.

Chef's Note: Rinsing Onions
One thing I learned growing up in Argentina was to always rinse diced or sliced raw onions before using them. Washing removes the strong-tasting juices given off when the onion is cut, making it milder and less prone to spoilage.

Tiraditos de Lenguado
with Aji Panca

The word tiraditos *means "ribbons" or "strips" in Spanish. It has become the latest rage in ceviches, inspired by Japanese sashimi. Here I use fluke, also called summer flounder because it comes close to shore during the summer and in most areas retreats to deeper, warmer waters for the winter. The firm, white, mild-flavored flesh makes it ideal for this dish and other ceviches. It also has the advantage of being readily available in fish markets up and down the East Coast. Sand dab would be a good West Coast substitute.*

Aji panca—the Peruvian word for chile is aji—*is known in Mexico and the Caribbean as* chile rojo seco *(dried red chile). It is brick-colored, fruity in flavor, and relatively mild in heat.*

SERVES 2

6 ounces skinless, center-cut
fluke fillet

¼ cup fresh lime juice

2 teaspoons kosher salt

2 tablespoons aji panca purée
(see Special Ingredients)

2 tablespoons olive oil

¼ cup water

2 tablespoons fresh cilantro leaves

■ Wrap the fluke in plastic wrap and freeze for about 30 minutes, or until firm and somewhat stiff. Using a very sharp knife, slice the fluke against the grain into thin, ribbon-shaped strips. Arrange the strips in parallel lines on a serving platter.

■ Mix the lime juice with 1 teaspoon salt and rub lightly into the fish. Cover and refrigerate for 30 minutes to cure.

■ In a blender jar, combine the panca purée, olive oil, water, and remaining teaspoon of salt. Blend to a smooth purée; then scrape into a zipper-lock freezer bag. Cut a very small section off one corner of the bag to form an opening. Test by squeezing out a little purée. If necessary, cut off a little more of the bag to create a larger opening. Squeeze small dots of the purée in a row across each strip of fish. Place a cilantro leaf in the center of each strip for garnish. Serve immediately, or cover and refrigerate for up to 2 hours before serving.

Fluke or Summer Flounder

Fluke, *Paralichthys dentatus*, is a member of the large family of thin, flat, bottom-swimming flatfish that includes flounder, halibut, and sole. Whole fluke, which generally weigh between two and five pounds, should have red, alive-looking gills and bright, unmarred skin. While summer fluke and winter flounder are closely related, the fluke has a large mouth full of teeth, while the flounder's mouth is small without visible teeth. At ¡Pasion! I am able to get excellent-quality fluke because so much of it is caught right off the New Jersey coast, not far from the restaurant.

Lenguado Handroll

with Green Mango Escabeche

This is ¡Pasion!'s take on the popular Japanese sushi bar handroll. Instead of covering the lenguado—the Spanish word for "sole"—with a thin layer of nori seaweed, I use whole cilantro leaves. In place of the pink pickled ginger that is a ubiquitous condiment for sushi, I serve pickled, paper-thin slices of green (unripe) mango in a South American flavor combo of lime, garlic, and fiery habanero chile. Every time I offer this dish, my kitchen staff quietly curse me because the rolls require a bit of handwork and are so popular that the staff can't stop rolling all night. I've since learned that if we make the rolls early in the evening and cover them with dampened paper towels, they keep beautifully for several hours. Using this method, you can serve them as a fresh, clean-tasting first course for a sit-down dinner party, or present them on a large tray as an hors d'oeuvre for a buffet meal.

—————————————————————————————— SERVES 4

4 thin, skinless flounder fillets, about ½ pound

¼ cup fresh lime juice

2 teaspoons kosher salt

2 tablespoons fresh cilantro leaves

1 firm but ripe Hass or Pinkerton avocado, peeled, trimmed to flatten edges, and cut into sticks

½ English cucumber, lightly peeled and cut into sticks

2 ripe plum tomatoes, seeded and cut into fillets

½ bunch fresh chives, cut into 3-inch lengths, plus 8 whole chives for tying

2 tablespoons wasabi powder

½ small habanero chile, seeded and finely chopped

½ cup Green Mango Escabeche (see recipe on page 162)

¼ cup soy sauce, for dipping

■ Arrange the flounder fillets on a clean work surface. Cover with plastic wrap and pound lightly, using the side of a heavy chef's knife. Combine the lime juice and salt. Transfer the pounded flounder to a nonreactive (stainless-steel or enameled) tray and sprinkle with the lime-and-salt mixture. Cover and refrigerate for about 30 minutes, or until the fillets are nearly opaque.

■ Remove the flounder from the marinade and place on a clean work surface, with the outer side of the fish down. Cut each flounder fillet into a 4-inch length, discarding the trimmings.

■ Cover the exposed inner side of the fish with a layer of cilantro leaves. Over the cilantro, on one short end of each of the flounder pieces, place one-quarter of the avocado, cucumber, tomato, and chives. Roll the fish up as tightly as possible around the vegetables, and repeat with remaining ingredients. Cover and refrigerate briefly to firm the rolls. Using a sharp knife, slice each roll crosswise into 2 pieces, and tie to secure with a chive. Place the rolls on a tray covered with plastic wrap or waxed paper, cover with a dampened paper towel, and refrigerate until ready to serve, up to 6 hours ahead.

■ In a small bowl, mix the wasabi and chile with enough water to make a thick, stiff paste. Form the paste into four marble-size balls and reserve. To serve the handrolls, place 2 pieces on each of 4 small serving plates. Garnish with a portion of the wasabi paste and a small mound of Green Mango Escabeche, and serve with a small dipping bowl of soy sauce.

Red Snapper Ceviche with Avocado Mash,
Tobiko Wasabi Vinaigrette

The magnificent red snapper, Lutjanus campechanus, *is sought after for ceviche in the Caribbean because of its fine texture and delicate flavor. Red snapper's closest cousin in appearance is the vermilion or B-line snapper, which is not as highly prized. True red snapper has a smaller eye and is not football-shaped like the vermilion snapper, which rarely exceeds four pounds. Most of our red snappers come from the Gulf Coast, often caught near the reefs where they tend to gather. Here I enhance this delicious fish with vinaigrette made with tobiko wasabi, a pale green, assertively flavored form of the flying fish roe so familiar from its use as a garnish for sushi.*

SERVES 4

1½ pounds whole red snapper, filleted, with skin on and pin bones removed (about ¾ pound fillet)

6 tablespoons fresh lime juice

2 teaspoons kosher salt

1 (3- to 4-inch) section daikon radish, peeled

1 firm but ripe avocado, preferably Hass

½ cup Tobiko Wasabi Vinaigrette (see recipe on page 157)

2 tablespoons red bell pepper, cut into diamond shapes

1 ounce tobiko caviar

■ Cut the red snapper fillet on the diagonal into thin strips, and place in a nonreactive (stainless-steel or enameled) bowl. (See Cutting Red Snapper for Ceviche, page 34, for complete directions.) Mix together ¼ cup lime juice and 1 teaspoon salt. Rub lightly into the fish slices. Cover and refrigerate for 30 minutes.

■ Shred or julienne the daikon, or cut into thin curls with a Benriner cutter, and place in a bowl of cold water.

■ Just before serving, cut the avocado in half lengthwise. Twist the halves in opposite directions until one side pops off. Remove the pit; then use a spoon to scoop out the avocado flesh. Place the avocado in a small bowl, add the remaining lime juice and salt, and mash with a fork.

■ To serve, roll up the snapper loosely and arrange the rolls in 4 chilled, open-necked stem glasses or ceramic bowls. Drizzle with the Tobiko Wasabi Vinaigrette.

■ Scoop a rounded spoonful of the avocado mash into one teaspoon. Use a second teaspoon to form it into an egg shape, and place on top of 1 roll of fish. Continue until each fish roll has been topped with an avocado "egg." Place 1 red pepper diamond on top of the avocado and surround with about ¼ teaspoon of tobiko caviar. Drain the shredded daikon, and garnish each serving with a small mound. Serve immediately.

Daikon Radish

This traditional Japanese vegetable, a smooth-fleshed, white-skinned winter radish, is often found in Asian markets. Also known as oriental, Japanese, or giant white radish, it is commonly pickled or grated and used as a garnish. Its color can range from white to pink to black to green. The variety most commonly available is about 1 foot long and 1 to 4 inches in diameter. Before grating or shredding, scrub or peel the daikon, removing only a thin layer of skin. It is the ideal vegetable for one of those fancy Japanese Benriner cutters, sold in many Asian markets, that make long, spaghetti-shaped vegetable curls.

Red Snapper Ceviche
with Lamb Tongue Salad

Here I was inspired to combine somewhat gamy spiced lamb tongue with delicate, sweet red snapper, one of the premier fish of the Caribbean. I wasn't sure if this dish would sell, but it turned out to be a surprise hit. The contrasting flavors and textures of the fish and the lamb work beautifully together. You will need to start the tongue a week ahead of time to allow it to pickle properly.

SERVES 6

¾ pound skinless red snapper fillet, cut across the grain into thin slices (see Cutting Red Snapper for Ceviche)

1 recipe (¾ cup) Basic Ceviche Marinade (see recipe on page 182)

1 cup Slow-Roasted Beets, cut into ½-inch dice (see recipe on page 187)

3 tablespoons extra virgin olive oil

3 tablespoons fresh lemon juice

2 tablespoons chiffonade of Italian parsley

1½ teaspoons kosher salt

½ teaspoon freshly ground black pepper

1 Lamb Tongue in Escabeche (see recipe on page 163), sliced paper thin

■ Arrange the snapper slices in a non-reactive (stainless-steel or enameled) pan in a single layer and pour the Basic Ceviche Marinade over them. Cover and refrigerate for 30 minutes.

■ In a small bowl, combine the beets, olive oil, lemon juice, 1 tablespoon Italian parsley, 1 teaspoon salt, and ¼ teaspoon pepper. Toss the sliced lamb tongue with the remaining tablespoon of parsley and the remaining salt and pepper.

■ Remove the snapper from the marinade and arrange in a fan shape on 6 individual serving plates. At the point of the fan, place a small mound of the beets and top with a portion of the lamb tongue. Drizzle a little of the snapper marinade over the fish and serve immediately.

Cutting Red Snapper for Ceviche

To cut the red snapper for ceviche, wrap the fillet in plastic wrap and freeze for about 30 minutes, or until firm and somewhat stiff. Firmly grasp the tail end of the fish with one hand. Using a very sharp knife and starting at the tail, cut the flesh away from the skin while pulling the skin in the opposite direction. Discard the skin. Cut away and discard the strip of dark flesh that runs down the center of the fish.

You will now have 2 fillets of snapper. The top loin (cut from the upper side of the fish) will be thicker. Using a very sharp knife, cut straight across the top loin, starting from the head end and continuing about three-quarters of the way down the fillet. Discard the tail end of the fillet, which is too stringy to use. Starting at the head end, cut the bottom loin into slightly thicker, angled slices against the grain of the fish.

Big-Eye Tuna Ceviche with Roasted Calabaza,
Tuna Caviar Vinaigrette

This ceviche combines big-eye tuna (called ahi *in sushi bars, where it is a favorite) with South American calabaza squash and popped pumpkin seeds. The* bottarga *is tuna roe that has been salted and pressed to create a strongly flavored condiment. The best pumpkin seed oil comes not from the Americas, as you might expect, but from the Austrian Tyrol, where special varieties of pumpkin are raised for their seed oil. For this recipe, you'll need four 3-inch ring molds or biscuit cutters, or you can improvise by using four washed-out tuna cans with both ends removed.*

SERVES 4

TUNA CEVICHE

1 teaspoon tuna caviar (bottarga)
    or ground dried shrimp
    (see Special Ingredients)
¼ cup extra virgin olive oil
¼ cup fresh lemon juice
¼ cup fresh lime juice
2 tablespoons pumpkin seed oil,
    preferably Austrian
    (see Special Ingredients)
1 pound sushi-grade big-eye tuna
    (also called ahi) trimmed and cut
    into ½-inch dice
¼ cup Popped Pepitas (see recipe
    on page 148)
1 tablespoon thinly sliced
    garlic chives
Kosher salt and freshly ground
    black pepper to taste

■ In the jar of a blender (or in a bowl with an immersion blender), combine the tuna caviar, olive oil, lemon juice, lime juice, and pumpkin seed oil. Blend until well combined and creamy.

Remove from blender and reserve ¼ cup. Scrape the remaining mixture into a medium bowl. Add the tuna, Popped Pepitas, garlic chives, salt, and pepper, and fold gently to combine.

ROASTED CALABAZA

1 pound calabaza squash, peeled,
    seeded, and cut into ¾-inch dice
2 tablespoons olive oil
Salt and freshly ground pepper
    to taste

■ Preheat the oven to 425°F. Toss the squash, oil, and seasonings in a bowl. Spread in a single layer on a baking pan. Roast 15 to 20 minutes, shaking and tossing once or twice, until the squash is browned and crusty on the outside and soft on the inside. Remove from oven and cool, cover, and then refrigerate until chilled.

PEPPERCRESS SALAD

1 tablespoon pumpkin seed oil,
    preferably Austrian
    (see Special Ingredients)
¼ cup lemon juice
¼ cup lime juice
Kosher salt and freshly ground
    black pepper to taste
½ pound peppercress leaves
    (or watercress leaves)

■ Combine the oil, lemon juice, lime juice, and seasonings. Toss lightly with the cress. Place one ring mold on each of 4 chilled salad plates. Divide the roasted calabaza among the molds, pressing down lightly. Divide the tuna mixture among the rings, and press down lightly to shape. Remove the rings and top each portion with one-quarter of the peppercress salad. Drizzle the reserved vinaigrette over each plate and serve immediately.

Big-Eye Tuna Ceviche Picadillo
with Maduros

Picadillo *comes from the Spanish verb* picar, *to cut into small pieces. In culinary terms, it is a mixture of meat with aromatics such as onion and garlic, and bold flavors such as cumin and sherry vinegar. It often includes raisins or currants for a bit of sweetness, and toasted almonds or pine nuts for crunch. Here the picadillo is made with small dice of fresh, raw big-eye tuna. The sauce recipe yields three cups. Use the remaining sauce to make a terrific vinaigrette.*

SERVES 4

PICADILLO SAUCE

1 green bell pepper, seeded
   and chopped
½ Spanish onion, peeled and diced
1 clove garlic
½ cup fresh lime juice
2 cups tomato purée
   (preferably Pomi brand)
1 tablespoon ground cumin
½ cup Amontillado sherry
1 cup tomato juice
½ cup extra virgin olive oil
3 tablespoons kosher salt

■ Combine all the ingredients in a blender jar and blend until smooth.

MADUROS

2 very ripe, black-skinned plantains
½ cup olive oil
½ teaspoon kosher salt

■ Just before serving, peel the plantains. Trim off and discard the ends. Cut the plantains on a diagonal into ¾-inch-thick slices. Heat the oil in a heavy cast-iron or nonstick skillet until shimmering. Add the plantain slices and brown well on one side. Using a slotted spatula, because the maduros are quite soft, turn over the slices. Brown well on the second side. Using the slotted spatula, remove from the pan and arrange on paper towels to drain briefly. Sprinkle with kosher salt.

TUNA CEVICHE

¾ pound sushi-grade ahi or big-eye
   tuna, cut into ¼-inch dice
3 tablespoons sliced almonds,
   lightly toasted
2 teaspoons Zante currants
   (or dark raisins)
2 teaspoons chopped Italian parsley
2 tablespoons pitted green olives,
   sliced
1 cup Picadillo Sauce

■ In a medium nonreactive (stainless-steel or enameled) bowl, combine the tuna, almonds, currants, Italian parsley, olives, and Picadillo Sauce. Taste for seasoning. Divide between 4 salad plates and serve immediately, surrounded with the maduros.

Picadillo Vinaigrette

To 1½ cups Picadillo Sauce, add 3 tablespoons sherry vinegar and an additional ½ cup extra virgin olive oil. Pour into the jar of a blender and blend until smooth and creamy. Use this flavorful, assertive vinaigrette to dress salads of robust greens like arugula and Belgian endive.

Fresh Smoked Salmon Ceviche,

Grilled Corn and Huitlacoche Vinaigrette

In this recipe, I explain how to use very low-tech materials, such as a cardboard box, to make a cold smoker. Hot smoking actually cooks the fish, while cold smoking simply imparts flavor without changing the lush texture of the raw flesh. The fancy cold-smoked salmon imported from Canada, Scotland, and Ireland is cured in brine before being cold-smoked. This brine preserves the fish but imparts a stronger taste. Here, instead of using brine, I spice the salmon to add a lively Latino flavor.

SERVES 8

FRESH SMOKED SALMON

2 tablespoons kosher salt

2 tablespoons sugar

2 tablespoons paprika

1 tablespoon chile ancho powder
   (see Special Ingredients)

1 teaspoon chipotle powder
   (see Special Ingredients)

1 (2- to 2½-pound) skinless salmon
   fillet in one piece

■ In a small bowl, combine the salt, sugar, paprika, ancho powder, and chipotle powder, mixing well. Rub all over the fish, cover, and refrigerate for 2 hours. Have ready a cold-smoking assembly, following the directions in Chef's Techniques on page 15, and heat the wood chips as directed.

■ Remove the fish from the refrigerator and place it on the top wire rack. Position the rack so that it rests on the metal bowl of ice. Close the lid of the box, and smoke for 30 minutes. Open the box, remove the rack with

the fish, and discard the water in the bowl. Fill the bowl with ice again, replace the rack with the fish, close the lid, and smoke for 30 minutes more. The smoke should never be thick and white, an indication that the temperature is too high. You should just be able to see thin strands of smoke escaping.

■ Remove the fish from the smoker, cover, and refrigerate about 1 hour until cold, or up to 2 weeks. You will have enough smoked salmon to serve 12 to 16 people. Use about half the salmon for this recipe, which serves six. The remaining smoked salmon will keep well, covered and refrigerated, for about 2 weeks.

ASSEMBLING THE SALMON CEVICHE

1 cup Grilled Corn Salsa
   (see recipe on page 152)

½ cup Huitlacoche Vinaigrette
   (see recipe on page 153)

■ To serve, cut the salmon thinly across the grain into 24 to 30 thin slices. Form 6 rosettes by wrapping 4 to 5 slices of salmon, one around the other, to resemble a rose with partially open petals. Place a mound of Grilled Corn Salsa on each of 6 serving plates. Cover with a salmon rosette. Dot the Huitlacoche Vinaigrette around the edge of the plate. Serve immediately.

Huitlacoche

Considered a delicacy in Mexican cuisine, huitlacoche is a fungus that grows inside corn kernels. The purple-black fungus is visible through the distended and translucent skin of the kernels. It has an earthy, slightly sweet flavor reminiscent of truffles and black trumpet mushrooms. The name *huitlacoche* comes from an Aztec word, and the fungus was prized in both the Aztec and the Mayan cultures. Although it is available canned, I only use the fresh product.

Salmon Ceviche with Pink Peppercorns,
Mixed Seaweed Salad

Thinly sliced salmon, pink peppercorns, and Japanese mixed seaweeds come together in this simple, visually appealing dish, which can be assembled in twenty minutes. I buy the dried, shredded seaweed, a combination of five different seaweeds of various colors, from a Japanese importer. To reconstitute, it only needs to be soaked in water for five minutes. A creamy sour-cream-and-onion sauce is the perfect complement.

SERVES 4

SEAWEED SALAD

1 ounce (⅓ package) mixed dried, shredded seaweed (see Special Ingredients)

2 jalapeño chiles, seeded and minced

3 tablespoons soy sauce

1 tablespoon Japanese roasted sesame oil

2 teaspoons miso

1 teaspoon *sambal oelek* (Indonesian red chile paste) (see Special Ingredients)

2 tablespoons olive oil

1 teaspoon kosher salt

¼ teaspoon freshly ground black pepper

■ Soak the seaweed in a bowl of cold water for 5 minutes. Drain and squeeze out excess liquid. Combine the jalapeños, soy sauce, sesame oil, miso, sambal oelek, olive oil, salt, and black pepper, and blend to make a creamy dressing. Mix with the seaweed and reserve, refrigerated, for up to 1 hour.

SALMON AND SAUCE

¾ pound sushi-grade salmon fillet

¼ cup sour cream

½ cup finely diced onion, rinsed

½ cup fresh lime juice

1 tablespoon kosher salt

1 teaspoon sambal oelek (Indonesian red chile paste) (see Special Ingredients)

¼ cup water

2 teaspoons olive oil

1 teaspoon pink peppercorns

■ Slice the salmon thinly against the grain into about 24 thin scallops. Place a mound of the seaweed salad in the center of 4 individual serving plates. Form 4 rosettes by wrapping 6 slices of salmon decoratively, one around the other, to form a rose with partially open petals. Place one of the rosettes on each plate. Whisk together the sour cream, onion, lime juice, salt, sambal oelek, water, and olive oil. Drizzle each plate with this sauce and crumble the pink peppercorns on top.

Miso

There are many types of miso, each with its own aroma, flavor, color, and texture. All are made by essentially the same method. First, boiled soybeans are crushed and wheat, barley, or rice is added. Then the mixture is injected with a yeastlike mold and allowed to mature for months, or up to 3 years. Here I use light, yellow miso, injected with rice mold, which is relatively sweet and very good for dressings.

Pink Peppercorns

Also known as "pepper roses," pink peppercorns have a bittersweet, mild aroma rather than a spicy flavor. They aren't peppercorns at all, but the dried berry of an entirely different plant, *Schinus molle*, from the French island of Reunion, near Madagascar. Use pink peppercorns with discretion, because a little goes a long way.

Ceviche de los Enamorados

This is truly a dish for lovers (enamorados), *because of the passionate red color of the salmon and the salmon caviar. The theme continues with the dramatic color of Blood Orange Sauce flavored with passion fruit purée, then topped with the fresh fruit pulp still bearing its crunchy, nutlike seeds. I serve this ceviche with a Rum Negroni sugar cane stick for an unexpected but wholly appropriate garnish. To appreciate sugar cane fully, suck and then chew the sticks to extract the delectable cane syrup inside. Of course, you'll want to drink Rum Negroni cocktails.*

SERVES 2

1 3- to 4-inch length fresh sugar cane
(see Special Ingredients)
1 cup Rum Negroni (see recipe on
page 174)
¼ cup Blood Orange Sauce
(see recipe on page 155)
½ pound sushi-grade salmon fillet,
cut into cubes about ½ inch
in diameter
2 blood oranges, peeled and
cut into segments
1 fresh passion fruit, halved,
with pulp scooped out
1 tablespoon salmon caviar

■ Using a sharp, heavy knife, split the sugar cane lengthwise into sticks, as you would split logs of wood, ½ inch thick and 3 inches long. Marinate the sugar cane in the Rum Negroni for 20 minutes, then drain.

■ Combine the Blood Orange Sauce with the salmon cubes. Place in an attractive mound on each of 2 chilled serving plates. Arrange the orange segments in a circle surrounding the salmon. Top each portion with half of the passion fruit pulp, then half of the salmon caviar. Garnish with the sugar cane sticks.

Blood Oranges

First grown in Sicily in the seventeenth century, probably as a result of a chance mutation, blood oranges are extremely tart, with deep red pulp. There are two main varieties: the round Moros and the elongated Taroccos. Both have a complex, concentrated flavor with a slight edge of bitterness, making them excellent for both savory and sweet dishes. To find blood oranges with the most dramatic red flesh, look for fruits with the reddest skin. While they are now being grown in California, European varieties are still more colorful.

Passion Fruit

Passion fruit, *Passiflora edulis*, is a small, intoxicatingly fragrant tropical fruit that goes by many names in different parts of Latin America, including granadilla, parcha, and maracujá. The round or oval fruits are 1½ to 3 inches in length, with a tough, smooth, waxy rind ranging in color from dark purple to light yellow or pumpkin-orange. Inside is a mass of soft pulp filled with seeds. It is quite acidic, with a unique, powerful flavor that has been compared to guava and mango. Purple passion fruit is native to southern Brazil and northern Argentina. The yellow fruit is thought to be native to the Amazon region of Brazil.

Black Bass Ceviche,

Chayote Mirasol Salad

Here I use black sea bass, often served whole and steamed or deep-fried in many Chinese restaurants. I char the skin of the bass, making it good to eat instead of chewy and tough, as it is when raw. It's best to use a blowtorch from the hardware store or one of the small torches sold in kitchen supply stores, although you can also use the broiler. See page 165 for more information about chayote squash.

SERVES 4

1 pound black sea bass fillet, with
  skin on and pin bones removed
½ cup fresh lime juice
2 tablespoons soy sauce
Pinch salt
2 teaspoons Japanese roasted
  sesame oil
¼ chayote squash, unpeeled,
  with large seed cut out
1 (2-inch) section fresh ginger, peeled
2 scallions, green part only
1 whole fresh mirasol chile
  (see Special Ingredients)

■ Preheat the broiler (or use a small kitchen blowtorch). Place the sea bass fillet under the hot broiler for 1 to 2 minutes, only as long as it takes for the skin to get browned and bubbly. Remove the fillets from the broiler and wrap in plastic wrap. Freeze for about 30 minutes, or until firm and somewhat stiff. Using a very sharp knife, cut on the bias into ½-inch slices. Arrange in a single layer in a shallow, nonreactive (stainless-steel or enameled) bowl or platter.

■ In a small bowl, whisk the lime juice, soy sauce, salt, and sesame oil. Rub half of this marinade into the fish, cover, and refrigerate for 30 minutes.

■ Using a mandoline or a Benriner cutter, cut long julienne strips of the chayote and place in a bowl of cold water until ready to use. Using a sharp knife, cut the ginger into very fine julienne strips. Bring a small saucepan of water to the boil. Add the ginger and cook 1 minute. Drain in a colander and rinse under cold water to stop the cooking.

■ Cut the scallions into thin julienne strips. Trim and seed the chile, and cut into very thin julienne strips.

■ Combine the chayote, ginger, scallions, and chile with the remaining marinade. To serve, arrange sections of marinated sea bass in a circle in the center of 4 serving plates. Place a small mound of the salad on top. Drizzle the fish with any remaining dressing, and serve immediately.

Black Sea Bass

Black sea bass, *Centropristis striata,* is also known as blackfish. It has a double dorsal fin and broad vertical stripes with brownish gray to bluish black skin. Because the fish darkens when caught, it takes on an etched appearance due to scales that bleach instead of darkening. Ranging from 1½ to 5 pounds, it swims in deep water. At my restaurant, we buy black sea bass from fishermen who catch it off the New Jersey coast.

Mirasol Chiles

Mirasol chiles, which get their name from their habit of growing upward and "looking into the sun," have an earthy flavor with faint plum and raisin tones. Relatively mild, with a distinctive flavor, this thin-skinned chile can vary more than any other in looks and therefore may be difficult to recognize in its fresh state. It is very popular in Mexico.

Peruvian-Style Sea Trout Ceviche
with Grilled Cuzco Corn and Sweet Potato

For this classic Peruvian ceviche, with its requisite garnish of corn and sweet potato, I use sea trout, also known as weakfish. I buy frozen kernels of giant Cuzco corn from Peru for this dish. Canned white hominy is an acceptable substitute. Here I thread the cooked corn kernels on a bamboo skewer and then grill for a tasty and unusual garnish. Buy the black sesame seeds in Asian markets or from spice companies.

SERVES 4

½ pound skinless sea trout fillets

2 tablespoons rice wine vinegar

2 tablespoons soy sauce

¼ teaspoon sugar

¼ teaspoon *nanami togarashi*
   (see Special Ingredients)

1 teaspoon black sesame seeds

1 teaspoon grated fresh ginger

1 tablespoon fresh lime juice

2 large sweet potatoes, peeled,
   with 1 inch cut off the ends

1 teaspoon kosher salt

1 cup frozen Cuzco corn, defrosted
   (see Special Ingredients)

1 tablespoon vegetable oil,
   for grilling

■ Wrap the sea trout fillets in plastic wrap and freeze for about 30 minutes, or until firm and somewhat stiff. Using a very sharp knife, cut on the bias into very thin slices. Arrange in a single layer in a shallow bowl or platter.

■ In a small bowl, whisk together the rice wine vinegar, soy sauce, sugar, nanami togarashi, black sesame seeds, ginger, and lime juice. Rub this marinade into the fish, cover, and refrigerate for 30 minutes.

■ Cut a thin slice off one side of each sweet potato so that it sits flat. Cut crosswise into ½-inch-thick slabs. Stack the slabs evenly and cut into 1-inch-wide sticks. Bring a medium saucepan of water to the boil with the salt. Add the sweet potato sticks and cook 5 minutes, or until tender but still firm. Using a slotted spoon or wire skimmer, remove from the water. Rinse under cool (not cold) water, and drain.

Weakfish

"Weakies," *Cynoscion regalis*, are commonly known as sea trout, although this is a misnomer. They are members of the drum or croaker family, which get their name from the males' ability to make a loud drumming noise in the water using their croaking muscles. The term *weakfish* derives from the soft mouths of the fish. Line fishermen often lose the fish because the hook tends to tear loose from its mouth. Weakfish is an excellent, mild-flavored, white-fleshed fish that is generally inexpensive and relatively easy to find in retail fish markets. It resembles a fat, greenish brown trout and has a silvery body with a dense pattern of small, dark spots. Weakfish swim in schools from Massachusetts in the summer down to Florida in colder weather. The flesh is lean and flaky but can feel flabby if the fish is less than fresh.

■ Preheat a grill to very high heat. Thread the corn onto 4 bamboo skewers. (You'll have extra corn, so don't be concerned if you break a few kernels trying to thread them.) Brush the skewers with a little of the oil, and grill on both sides until blackened grill marks are formed. Brush the sweet potato sticks with oil. Place the sticks atop the grill on the diagonal and grill; then turn 90 degrees and grill again to form diamond-shaped grill marks on one side. It is not necessary to grill on both sides.

■ To serve the ceviche, arrange the marinated sea trout slices, with their marinade, in parallel rows on 4 serving plates. Garnish each plate with 1 corn skewer and 3 or 4 sweet potato slices, each placed in the opposite direction from the one below. Serve immediately.

Nanami Togarashi

Nanami togarashi is a Japanese chile-and-spice mix that contains hot chile powder, dried orange peel, sesame seeds, seaweed, and other spices. I buy it in Asian markets and favor the S & B brand. It's quite pungent, so use it in small quantities.

Bonito Ceviche with Grilled Nopalitos,
Melon Salsa

Here I use bonito, one of the smaller members of the huge family of fish that includes tuna and mackerel. I marinate the bonito in a dressing with Japanese flavors and combine it with grilled cactus paddles, nopales or nopalitos in Spanish. The sweet melon salsa is a palate refresher that also makes for a juicy ceviche.

SERVES 6

MELON SALSA

¼ honeydew melon, firm but ripe, peeled

¼ Crenshaw or Persian melon, firm but ripe, peeled

¼ cup fresh lime juice

½ guajillo chile, sliced paper-thin (see Special Ingredients)

2 teaspoons kosher salt

■ Trim both melons into fairly even rectangles. Cut into ½-inch slices, then cut crosswise into ½-inch-wide sticks, and finally cut into cubes. Whisk together the lime juice, chile, and salt, and toss with the melons. Cover and refrigerate for 30 minutes before serving to allow the salsa to macerate.

GRILLED NOPALITOS

2 large, firm cactus paddles

1 tablespoon vegetable oil

1 teaspoon kosher salt

■ Take care when handling the cactus paddles, because they may have strong, sharp thorns. Before using, shave off the thorns with a vegetable peeler. Trim off the tough outer edges of the paddles. Toss the trimmed nopalitos with the oil and salt.

■ Preheat a grill until very hot. Grill the paddles on both sides until lightly charred. Cool slightly; then cut into thin strips.

Nopalitos

In many Latin cultures, people greatly enjoy eating cactus leaves. Called *nopales* (or the diminutive *nopalitos*) in Spanish, these fleshy, oval leaves come from the nopal, or prickly pear cactus. They are becoming more readily available in the United States, especially in areas with large Mexican and other Hispanic populations. Eaten as a vegetable, nopales have a delicate, slightly tart flavor. Some say they taste a bit like asparagus or green beans. Succulent yet crisp, they can exude a sticky substance like okra when cooked. Choose small, firm, pale green nopales with no signs of wrinkling. Here, because I grill the nopalitos, they remain firm without stickiness.

BONITO CEVICHE

1 pound skinless bonito fillet

2 tablespoons rice wine vinegar

2 tablespoons soy sauce

2 teaspoons sugar

2 teaspoons Japanese roasted
   sesame oil

1 tablespoon grated fresh ginger

2 tablespoons chopped fresh cilantro

¼ cup chopped roasted,
   salted peanuts

■ Cut the bonito into slices 1 inch thick. Slice crosswise to ⅜ inch; then cut again into short sticks. Cover and refrigerate until ready to serve. In a small bowl, whisk together the vinegar, soy sauce, sugar, sesame oil, ginger, cilantro, and peanuts, and reserve.

■ When ready to serve, toss the soy sauce mixture with the bonito, and spoon on one end of a shallow oval serving bowl. Spoon the melon salsa into the center of the bowl. Place the grilled nopalitos at the other end, and serve immediately.

Bonito

The Pacific bonito, *Sarda chiliensis,* is one of the smaller fish in the huge family of Scombridae, which includes mackerel and tuna. Its body is cigar-shaped, and its head pointed and conical, with a large mouth. The Pacific bonito is dark blue on top, dusky on the sides, and silvery below. A number of dark stripes slant along its back. The fish can be found in waters from Chile to the Gulf of Alaska. The rich, oily flesh resembles that of mackerel.

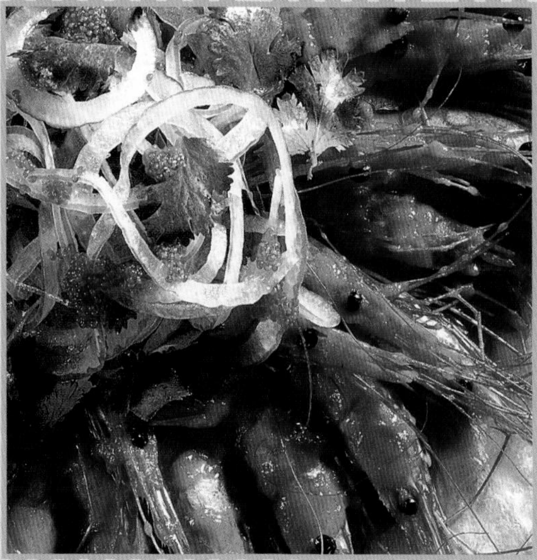

RAW SEAFOOD

CEVICHE

Bay Scallop Ceviche,

Blackened Tomatillo–Truffle Sauce

This dish is one of my all-time favorite creations. The flavors just make magic together. I like to serve it as an hors d'oeuvre at stand-up cocktail parties. I place a mouthful of ceviche on a nonaluminum serving spoon, then top it at the last minute with a few crumbs of crunchy fried plantains. For a great presentation, serve the ceviche on Chinese ceramic soup spoons. You could also present it as a first course in small bowls. While I prefer to use my own homemade Platano Chips, you could use the packaged chips produced by Hispanic companies such as Goya.

SERVES 4 AS AN APPETIZER OR 12 AS AN HORS D'OEUVRE

BLACKENED TOMATILLO–TRUFFLE SAUCE

3 tablespoons extra virgin olive oil

½ pound fresh tomatillos, husks removed and rinsed

½ pound ripe plum tomatoes

1 red onion, quartered and unpeeled

1 jalapeño chile

4 cachucha chiles (see Special Ingredients)

1 bunch fresh cilantro leaves

½ cup fresh lime juice

3 tablespoons truffle oil

Kosher salt and freshly ground black pepper, to taste

■ In a large sauté pan, heat 1 tablespoon of the olive oil over moderately high heat. Add the tomatillos, tomatoes, onion, jalapeño, and cachuchas. Cook, tossing frequently, until the skins are blackened. Remove from the pan and cool to room temperature. Stir in the cilantro. For the best texture, use a meat grinder with a medium blade to grind the mixture. Otherwise, place the mixture in the bowl of a food processor and pulse briefly until the vegetables are chopped but still chunky.

■ Combine the vegetable mixture with the lime juice, truffle oil, remaining 2 tablespoons olive oil, salt, and pepper. Taste for seasoning, cover, and refrigerate for up to 1 day.

BAY SCALLOP CEVICHE

1 cup fresh lime juice

¼ cup fresh orange juice

3 tablespoons finely diced red onion

2 tablespoons finely diced serrano chiles (see Special Ingredients)

1 tablespoon kosher salt

1 pound fresh, untreated bay scallops (or sea scallops, trimmed and quartered)

2 tablespoons crushed Platano Chips (see recipe on page 136), for garnish

12 whole Platano Chips

■ In a nonreactive (stainless-steel or enameled) bowl, combine the lime juice, orange juice, onion, serrano chiles, and salt. Add the bay scallops and toss to combine. Cover and refrigerate for 24 hours. Drain off and discard all liquid.

■ In a medium bowl, combine the marinated scallops with most of the Blackened Tomatillo–Truffle Sauce. Cover and refrigerate 20 minutes to marinate. When ready to serve, drain the scallops of excess liquid, and toss with the remaining Blackened Tomatillo–Truffle Sauce. Adjust the seasoning, adding salt and pepper if necessary. Divide the ceviche among soup spoons laid on a platter. Sprinkle with crushed plantain chips just before serving, accompanied by bowls of plantain chips.

Yucatán Cocktail

Serve this "cocktail" in beautiful martini glasses and pretend you're on Isla Mujeres (Island of the Women) off the coast of Yucatán, where I first tasted the sublime combination. I always butterfly shrimp so they cook evenly. Make sure to use pink or white shrimp rather than the less expensive but often mushy warm-water tiger shrimp. Cotuit oysters from Cape Cod or Long Island Select oysters would be good here.

SERVES 4

12 large shrimp (21–25 count)

2 cups Basic Braising Liquid
(see recipe on page 182)

2 cups Pico de Gallo Salsa
(see recipe on page 152)

2 tablespoons aged tequila

12 medium shucked oysters

1 firm but ripe Hass or Pinkerton
avocado, peeled and cut into
large dice

12 Platano Chips (see recipe on
page 136)

4 curls Fresh Coconut Shavings
(see recipe on page 146)

■ Peel the shrimp, leaving the tail section intact, and cut them halfway down the backs to clean and butterfly. Remove and discard the dark vein running down the back. In a medium pot, bring the Basic Braising Liquid to the boil. Drop in the shrimp, stir, and cook only until opaque, about 2 minutes. Drain and rinse under cold water.

■ Combine the Pico de Gallo Salsa with the tequila. Add the shrimp, oysters, and avocado, and toss to combine. Divide between 4 chilled martini glasses and serve immediately, garnished with the Platano Chips and Fresh Coconut Shavings.

Shrimp

There are a vast number of different shrimp throughout the world, all divided into three basic categories: cold-water or northern; warm-water, tropical, or southern; and freshwater. I prefer the firm texture of cold-water shrimp to the mushier warm-water variety. By all means, avoid the black-shelled tiger shrimp sold inexpensively in many supermarkets, as they are too soft for ceviche. Cold-water shrimp from the northern Atlantic are called *Pandalus borealis,* while those that inhabit the northern Pacific are called *Pandalus jordoni.* Atlantic cold-water shrimp are found in northern waters from Alaska and Canada on the West Coast to Cape Cod, all the way to Greenland, and across the Atlantic to Norway.

Sea Scallop and Persimmon Ceviche,
Red Pearl Onion Escabeche

Here I combine a South American specialty, hearts of palm, with pickled pearl onions, sea scallops, and persimmons for a light, fruity ceviche. Start this simple dish at least one day ahead to allow time to marinate the scallops and prepare the Red Pearl Onion Escabeche. Do not use the treated scallops that have been soaked in a preservative liquid. Instead, ask your fishmonger for "dry-pack" scallops, which are untreated.

SERVES 4

½ pound fresh, untreated sea scallops, trimmed of hard adductor muscle

¾ cup Basic Ceviche Marinade (see recipe on page 182)

2 whole ripe persimmons, stem and large pit removed

1 cup Red Pearl Onion Escabeche with liquid (see recipe on page 161)

Kosher salt to taste

1 (14-ounce) can hearts of palm, drained and cut lengthwise into matchsticks

■ In a medium nonreactive (stainless-steel or enameled) bowl, combine the scallops and Basic Ceviche Marinade. Cover and refrigerate for 24 hours. Drain the scallops and slice each lengthwise into 2 to 3 thin rounds. Cover and refrigerate until ready to serve.

■ In a small bowl, mash the persimmon flesh until smooth. Add 3 tablespoons of liquid drained from the Red Pearl Onion Escabeche and stir to combine, adding kosher salt to taste. Add the hearts of palm and toss gently.

■ To assemble the ceviche, divide the marinated hearts of palm into 4 portions. Arrange on individual salad plates, creating a square "raft" of parallel strips placed side by side. Drizzle a bit of the persimmon marinade over the top.

■ Cut most of the drained Red Pearl Onion Escabeche into wedges and combine with the sliced scallops. Arrange the mixture on top of the hearts of palm and garnish each serving with the reserved whole pearl onions. Serve immediately.

Persimmons

Persimmons, *kaki* in Spanish, are extremely popular in South America. Persimmons are actually native to the eastern U.S., though the most popular commercial varieties, the large heart-shaped Fuyu and Hachiya, come from Japan. Before eating, persimmons must be practically wrinkled, extremely soft to the touch with clear, rather opaque flesh. An unripe persimmon is extremely unappealing, leaving your mouth with a puckery, fuzzy feeling. Sharon fruit is the name for the smaller, rounded variety of firm persimmon grown in Israel. Sharon fruit don't need to be fully ripened for you to enjoy them.

Sea Scallop Ceviche
with Ruby Grapefruit

Sea scallops are one of the easiest seafoods to prepare for ceviche, because all you need to do is remove the hard adductor muscle by which the scallop is attached to its shell. However, many scallops are treated with a liquid preservative to make them plumper. These should be avoided. Use only fresh, high-quality, untreated scallops for ceviche. If you have access to Nantucket bay scallops in season in October, try those exquisitely tender, sweet beauties in this dish. The slightly bitter yet sweet ruby grapefruit offsets the rich flavor of the scallops. Radishes are the perfect counterpoint to this quickly made ceviche.

SERVES 4

½ pound fresh untreated sea scallops, trimmed of hard adductor muscle

¾ cup Basic Ceviche Marinade (see recipe on page 182)

2 ruby grapefruits

6 red radishes, trimmed and thinly sliced

2 tablespoons fresh lime juice

¼ teaspoon hot red pepper flakes

½ teaspoon kosher salt

1 tablespoon fine chiffonade of Thai basil (or sweet basil)

1 tablespoon fine chiffonade of fresh mint

■ Slice each scallop lengthwise into 2 thin rounds. In a medium nonreactive (stainless-steel or enameled) bowl, toss the scallops with the Basic Ceviche Marinade. Cover and refrigerate for 30 minutes. Drain, cover, and refrigerate until ready to serve.

■ Using a sharp knife, cut away all of the skin and the thin outside layer of membrane enclosing the grapefruit sections. Cut out each section of fruit from between the membrane on both sides. Cut the radish slices into fine julienne.

■ In a medium nonreactive bowl, combine the lime juice, red pepper flakes, salt, basil, and mint. Reserve half the mixture. Toss the remaining lime juice mixture with the drained scallops. Toss the radish julienne with the reserved lime juice mixture.

■ Divide the scallops into 4 equal portions and arrange each portion on one side of 4 natural scallop shells or small salad plates. Next to the scallops, arrange the grapefruit segments, all facing the same direction, in a row. Place a small "haystack" of radish julienne between the scallops and the grapefruit. Serve immediately.

Ruby Grapefruit

The grapefruit, *Citrus paradisi*, was first found in Barbados during the 1750s and is a hybrid of the Pomelo, *Citrus grandis*, and the sweet orange, *Citrus sinensis*. The fruit got its name for the grape-like cluster in which it grows. Grapefruit seeds were brought from the Caribbean to South Texas by Spanish missionaries, and somewhere around 1929 a red grapefruit growing on a pink grapefruit trees was discovered. There are now Ruby Reds, Star Rubys, Flames, and Ruby Sweets available depending on the season. Choose firm grapefruits with a reddish blush to their skin.

Santa Barbara Spot Shrimp Ceviche,
Red Onion and Cilantro Salad

In summer these small, sweet shrimp, with black eyes protruding from their bodies, are shipped all the way from Santa Barbara, California. If the shrimp are still alive when I get them, I serve them raw. Otherwise I lightly cure them with lime juice and salt. They do not need to be deveined, but if you substitute other shrimp, be sure to devein them.

Rocoto is a popular Peruvian chile, which I buy already puréed and bottled. In Mexico, the same yellow chile is called chile manzano. It is medium in size, rounded, and plump, with a characteristic heart shape.

SERVES 8 TO 10

5 pounds whole Santa Barbara spot shrimp (substitute pink or white shrimp, not tiger shrimp)

1 cup fresh lime juice

4 teaspoons kosher salt

5 tablespoons rocoto purée (see Special Ingredients)

3 tablespoons Slow-Roasted Garlic Oil (see recipe on page 185)

2 tablespoons water

■ Peel the shells from the bodies of the shrimp, leaving their heads and the last segment of tail shells attached. In a large bowl, combine the lime juice with 1 tablespoon of salt. Add the shrimp and toss to combine. Cover and refrigerate for 30 minutes.

■ In a small bowl, whisk together the rocoto purée, Slow-Roasted Garlic Oil, water, and remaining teaspoon of salt to obtain a thick but pourable sauce. Drain the shrimp and arrange on a large platter in concentric circles with their heads facing inward. Drizzle the rocoto purée across the shrimp and serve, accompanied by the Red Onion and Cilantro Salad.

RED ONION AND CILANTRO SALAD

½ red onion, peeled and shaved into paper-thin rings

½ cup fresh cilantro leaves

½ teaspoon finely chopped garlic

2 tablespoons extra virgin olive oil

2 tablespoons fresh lime juice

1 teaspoon kosher salt

¼ teaspoon freshly ground black pepper

■ In a medium nonreactive (stainless-steel or enameled) bowl, combine all the ingredients and lightly toss. Serve the salad in a separate bowl to accompany the shrimp. Each guest takes a portion of shrimp and tops it with a little of the salad.

Santa Barbara Spot Shrimp

The Santa Barbara spot shrimp, *Pandalus platyceros*, also called California spot prawn, is named for the four bright white spots on its body located on both sides of the first and fifth shell segments. It is called *tarabaebi* in Japan, where it is a highly prized sushi bar item. Spot shrimp have pink to red shells with spots and sweet, firm flesh. Commonly found from Alaska to San Diego, spot prawns inhabit rocky areas. In Monterey, California, fishermen trap spot prawns all year. In southern California, trawlers fish for spot prawns during summer. If you find spot shrimp, look for the delicious roe under their belly shells. Use the roe as a garnish for the ceviche.

Oyster Ceviche,
Horseradish and English Cucumber Salad

Raw oysters and horseradish sauce are a classic "raw-bar" combo. Here I adapt the idea with a ceviche of oysters in fresh lime juice, mixed with small cubes of cucumber in horseradish sauce, and finished with a creamy beet salad. I happen to adore plain, ordinary saltine crackers, and I serve them here as a light, crunchy accompaniment. They are always served with ceviche in the Carribean. Use medium-sized oysters that can be eaten in one bite, the better to experience all the flavors and textures of the ceviche at once.

SERVES 4

16 freshly shucked oysters on the
   half shell (see To Open Oysters
   on page 70)
½ cup fresh lime juice
¼ cup finely diced Slow-Roasted
   Beets (see recipe on page 187)
½ teaspoon lime zest
   (green part only)
2 tablespoons sour cream
1 tablespoon water
1 teaspoon kosher salt
½ teaspoon freshly ground
   black pepper
½ cup peeled and finely diced
   English cucumber
1 tablespoon prepared white
   horseradish
16 saltine crackers

■ Sprinkle the oysters with half the lime juice, cover, and refrigerate for up to 2 hours. In a medium bowl, combine the beets, remaining lime juice, lime zest, sour cream, water, ½ teaspoon salt, and ¼ teaspoon pepper. Reserve.

■ Combine the cucumber with the horseradish and remaining salt and pepper. To serve, arrange 4 oysters on each of 4 chilled serving plates. Spoon about ½ teaspoon of the beet mixture on one end of each oyster. Spoon about ½ teaspoon of the cucumber mixture on the other end of the oyster. Serve immediately, encouraging your guests to pop the whole oyster and its garnishes into their mouths in one delicious bite. Serve the crackers on a separate plate so that they stay crisp.

Oysters

Now that so many oysters are farm-raised, they're available to us year-round. Buy oysters as fresh as possible from a reputable store with good turnover. Choose those with unbroken shells, and make sure they're all tightly closed. You can store oysters for two or three days in the refrigerator, with the larger shell down. Ideally, you'd wrap them in seaweed for storage, but covering them with a damp towel will do. Freshly shucked oysters covered by their own liquor will keep for up to a week when refrigerated. If you decide to shuck your own oysters (see page 70), take care to scrub the shells under cold, running water before opening them to avoid contaminating the oysters with exterior dirt or bacteria.

Oyster Ceviche
with Roasted Banana–Tamarindo Sauce, Tooloom Balls

This is one of my more involved recipes because it calls for lobster stock. The dish is outstanding, an unexpected layering of flavors, with roasted bananas, smoky chipotle chiles, and dark, tangy tamarind purée. Tamarind, also called Indian date, is the large fruit pod of a tamarind tree. The sour, prune-flavored pulp surrounding the seeds is widely used as a refreshing flavoring in South and Central America. The Tooloom Balls are made from a mixture of dried coconut, molasses, and a little dark rum.

You will need a ring mold to make neat shapes here. Improvise by using a small (about 1½ inch in diameter) biscuit cutter or a clean 6-ounce tuna can with the top and bottom removed.

SERVES 4

OYSTER CEVICHE WITH ROASTED BANANA–TAMARINDO SAUCE

3 yellow bananas

1 cup reduced Lobster Stock (see recipe on page 183)

2 tablespoons tamarind purée (see Chef's Techniques on page 14)

1 chipotle in adobo (see Special Ingredients)

1 teaspoon kosher salt

¼ cup lime juice

4 freshly shucked large oysters

12 Tooloom Balls

■ Preheat oven to 400°F. Place 1 whole banana in a baking dish and roast 20 minutes, or until the skin is dark brown and the banana is soft. Remove from oven, cool, and peel. Discard the peel and mash the pulp.

■ In a blender, combine the banana pulp, Lobster Stock, tamarind purée, chipotle, and salt. Purée until almost smooth, with a bit of texture remaining.

■ Peel and slice the remaining 2 bananas ¼ inch thick and toss with the lime juice. Drain the bananas and toss with about ¾ of the roasted banana–tamarind sauce. Divide into 4 portions. In parallel layers in the center of one of 4 serving plates, arrange the banana slices in the mold, forming a ring about 2 inches high. Unmold each banana ring carefully and drizzle with a little of the remaining sauce. Top with a single oyster. Arrange 3 Tooloom Balls on each plate and serve immediately.

TOOLOOM BALLS

MAKES 24 BALLS

¾ cup molasses

2 teaspoons grated fresh ginger

½ cup sugar

1½ cups dried coconut

Grated zest of 2 oranges

■ In a medium, heavy-bottomed pot, combine the molasses, ginger, sugar, 1 cup of the coconut, and orange zest. Bring to the boil, stirring constantly. Reduce heat to moderate and continue to cook until the mixture thickens and the sugar starts to caramelize, about 10 minutes. Remove from heat and cool. Scoop into balls with your fingers; then roll in remaining ½ cup coconut. The balls can be stored at room temperature in a covered container for up to 1 week.

Tooloom Balls

These molasses-flavored coconut balls are popular in Jamaica. Be sure to use plain molasses, available in natural foods stores; the darker blackstrap molasses is too strong for this dish. You can also buy dried, unsweetened coconut at natural foods stores. Do not use sweetened coconut for this dish.

Oyster Ceviche,
Smoked Jalapeño and Aguardiente Salsa

Here I use aguardiente, *a white, non-aged liquor that is often flavored with anise seeds. The word means "powerful." The brand I use, imported from Spain, is La Chinchonesa. Different versions of this potent spirit are produced throughout South America. Aguardiente is very popular in parts of Argentina and Colombia.*

The simple salsa topping for the oysters gets its special flavor from hot-smoked jalapeños. Serve with chilled shots of aguardiente as a chaser.

SERVES 4

4 jalapeño chiles

2 fresh unpeeled plum tomatoes, seeded and cut into tiny dice

2 tablespoons finely diced red onion, rinsed in cold water

½ teaspoon finely minced habanero chile

¼ cup fresh lime juice

1 teaspoon kosher salt

Very small pinch ground star anise (or ground toasted Spanish anise seeds)

1 tablespoon aguardiente

16 medium oysters on the half-shell

■ Following the method described on page 154 in the recipe for Smoked Corn–Amarillo Vinaigrette, hot-smoke the jalapeños for 20 minutes, or until the skins are dark olive in color and the chiles are soft.

■ Chill the smoked jalapeños in a bowl of ice water; then drain and rub off the skins. Cut the jalapeños open and scrape out the seeds and spongy white connective tissue. Cut the jalapeños into tiny dice.

■ In a medium bowl, combine the smoked jalapeños, diced tomatoes, onion, habanero, lime juice, salt, anise, and aguardiente to make a salsa. Arrange 4 oysters in each of 4 shallow serving bowls filled with crushed ice, top with the salsa, and serve immediately.

To Open Oysters

Using a heavy glove or dishcloth to protect your hand, turn each oyster so that its flat side is facing up and the pointed end is facing you. The pointed end curves slightly just beyond the tip, where the shells are joined. Put the oyster knife into that edge, just beyond the tip. Jiggle the knife until the blade slips inside.

Now twist vigorously to separate the shells, popping them apart. Scrape the knife across the inner shell to release the meat; then remove and discard the top shell. Scrape the knife against the inner bottom shell, cutting beneath the oyster to release it without piercing it. If you are using shucked oysters, remove each oyster from its shell, place in a clean container, and strain the juices through a sieve onto the oyster. If serving on the half-shell, give each opened oyster a quick rinse under cold water to remove any shell bits. Don't rinse more than necessary, to preserve the juices.

Tahitian-Style Abalone Ceviche

For this dish inspired by the South Pacific style of serving raw fish and seafood, I use live abalone in the shell. To continue the South Seas theme, I use fresh coconut, toasted cashews (actually native to Brazil), and tiny, flavorful dried shrimp, available in Asian markets. Because the shrimp are often a bit soggy, I toast them in a dry pan to crisp them up and release their pungent flavor. The rich, distinctive fragrance of fresh kaffir lime leaves mixes beautifully with the creamy coconut in this ceviche.

SERVES 4

COCONUT-LIME MARINADE

1 (14-ounce) can unsweetened
   coconut milk
¼ cup fresh lime juice
1 kaffir lime leaf, finely chopped
   (see Special Ingredients)
2 teaspoons chopped fresh ginger
2 teaspoons kosher salt

■ Combine the coconut milk, lime juice, lime leaf, ginger, and salt in a medium nonreactive (stainless-steel or enameled) saucepan. Bring to the boil; then lower the heat to moderate and cook for 20 minutes, or until thickened and reduced by half. Remove from the heat and strain through a fine-mesh sieve. Cover the marinade and refrigerate.

ABALONE CEVICHE

1 pound fresh abalone in the shell
   (see Special Ingredients)
2 tablespoons Fresh Coconut
   Shavings (see recipe on page 146)
2 teaspoons dried shrimp, lightly
   toasted in a dry pan
¼ cup roughly chopped roasted,
   salted cashews
4 teaspoons Pickled Pink Onions

(see recipe on page 163)
1 tablespoon chiffonade fresh cilantro

■ To clean the abalone, use a heavy spoon to dig under the smooth end and scoop it from the shell. Remove and discard the adductor muscle by which the abalone is attached. Cut the meat into thin slices and toss with the Coconut-Lime Marinade in a nonreactive (stainless-steel or enameled) bowl. Cover and refrigerate for at least 2 and up to 3 hours before serving. Scrub 4 abalone shells, dry, and reserve for serving.

■ When ready to serve, divide the abalone into 4 portions and spoon into reserved shells. Top each portion with 1½ teaspoons Fresh Coconut Shavings, ½ teaspoon dried shrimp, 1 tablespoon cashews, 1 teaspoon Pickled Pink Onions, and a little chiffonade cilantro. Serve immediately.

Abalone

California red abalone, *Haliotis rufescens*, is one of the rarest and most sought-after shellfish in the world. Several companies now raise and ship live abalone to restaurants and markets across the country. Though rather expensive, fresh abalone has a superb flavor, cream-colored meat, and a firm texture. It is prized for sushi and sashimi. Farm-raised abalones weigh, on average, about a quarter-pound in the shell.

Kaffir Lime Leaves

Grown in Southeast Asia and Hawaii, the kaffir lime tree, *Citrus hystrix*, produces small, pear-shaped fruit with a skin that's bright yellow-green, bumpy, and wrinkled. The glossy, dark leaves, used in cooking, have a unique double shape and look like two leaves joined end to end. Kaffir limes are valued for their zest and also for the marvelous perfume of the leaves. You can find dried kaffir lime rind and leaves in Asian markets. Fresh leaves, which have a more intense fragrance, are sometimes available from sources listed in Special Ingredients and Tools.

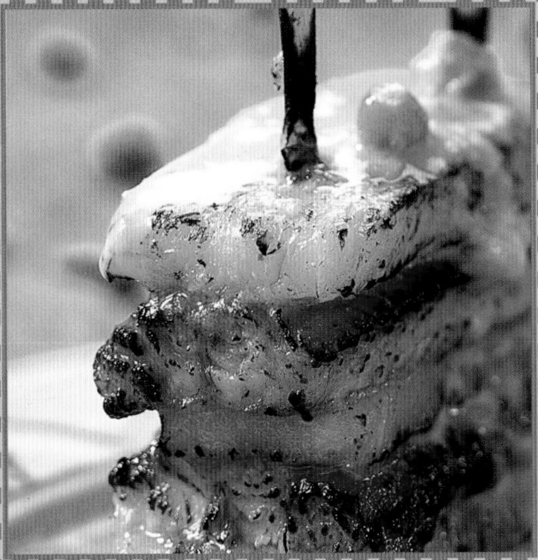

COOKED FISH

CEVICHE

Fresh Anchovy Ceviche,
Parsley Salad

In Spain, boquerones *is the word for this popular tapa, which has also become a favorite among South Americans. Fresh anchovies are a real delicacy. If you've only tasted the canned, oil-packed type, you've been missing out. To add a special salty crunch, I fry the anchovy spines and serve them as a garnish for this ceviche.*

SERVES 4

2 tablespoons extra virgin olive oil

1 tablespoon fresh lemon juice

Kosher salt and freshly ground black
  pepper to taste

½ pound marinated fresh anchovies,
  drained (see Special Ingredients)

½ cup Italian parsley leaves

¼ cup fine chiffonade of basil
  (or whole tiny basil leaves)

½ cup Crunchy Shallots (see recipe
  on page 136)

¼ cup lightly toasted sliced almonds

■ Whisk together the olive oil, lemon juice, a little salt, and plenty of black pepper. Arrange the anchovies in a sunburst pattern to cover a round or oval serving platter. In a small bowl, toss the Italian parsley, basil, and shallots with the olive oil dressing. Mound the herb salad in the center of the platter. Sprinkle with the almonds and serve immediately.

Fresh Anchovies

Anchovies are small, bright silver fish that swim in schools. The Mediterranean and Southern European coasts are home to so-called "true anchovy," *Ergraulis encrasicholus,* which has been prized since antiquity. Similar species are harvested along the Pacific and Atlantic coasts. Their intense, gutsy flavor is indispensable in cuisines around the world. They are particularly prized in Spain, in the delicate cured version called *boquerones,* sometimes available here at specialty markets. Anchovies have white, off-white, or grayish flesh with a smooth, fatty texture and rich flavor. Fresh anchovies are sold in certain fish markets, particularly those that cater to French, Spanish, and Portuguese customers. Unfortunately, rich, tiny fish like these go bad very quickly. A fresh anchovy will be silvery in color—not blue or dark.

Angulas Ceviche
with Malanga Chips

Eating angulas, *the tiny, almost transparent baby eels, is something of an obsession in Spain. While it's difficult to find fresh angulas in America, I serve them as often as I can at ¡Pasion!. Angulas are so tender that you need to shake rather than stir them while cooking to keep them intact. The chips that accompany this dish are made from taro or* malanga, *a starchy vegetable with lavender threads running through its white flesh.*

SERVES 4

¼ cup extra virgin olive oil
8 cloves garlic, peeled and
    thinly sliced
½ teaspoon hot red pepper flakes
½ pound fresh angulas
1 teaspoon kosher salt
½ cup Italian parsley leaves
¼ cup fresh lemon juice
Macerated Tomato Vinaigrette
24 Crispy Malanga Chips
    (see recipe on page 138)

■ In a medium, heavy-bottomed skillet, heat the olive oil, sliced garlic, and pepper flakes over moderate heat. Cook 2 to 3 minutes, or until the garlic has softened and is light golden in color. Drain the angulas and toss lightly with the salt. Add the angulas to the olive oil and cook over moderate heat, shaking the skillet occasionally, for about 1 minute, or until the angulas turn opaque white and curl up. Add the parsley leaves and lemon juice,

and shake the pan to combine well. Immediately remove from the heat and cool to room temperature.

■ To serve, spoon a pool of Macerated Tomato Vinaigrette on one side of 4 small plates. Place a portion of the angulas and pan juices alongside, and serve immediately, accompanied by the Crispy Malanga Chips.

MACERATED TOMATO VINAIGRETTE

4 halves Tomato Confit and liquid
    (see recipe on page 184)
2 tablespoons red wine vinegar
1 teaspoon kosher salt

■ Place the Tomato Confit and liquid, vinegar, and salt in the bowl of a food processor. Process to a chunky purée and reserve.

Angulas

Angulas, or baby eels, are a great delicacy to Spaniards and Italians, and can command an extremely high price. Their flavor is so subtle that it can easily be lost. Above all, they must be cooked briefly. In Spain, restaurants provide special angulas forks made of wood to avoid imparting any metallic taste. Ever since ancient Greece, people have been perplexed by the mysterious procreation of the eel. It was not until early this century that scientists discovered that female eels in Europe grow to adulthood in fresh water, and then meet the males at the mouths of rivers to mate. The females then embark on an amazing journey of more than four thousand miles across the Atlantic to the Sargasso Sea, between Bermuda and Puerto Rico, where they are caught in nets.

Curried King Mackerel Escabeche

I use natural jute twine to prepare this dish of hefty king mackerel steaks. Tying the mackerel helps keep its even shape while cooking, and the twine adds a rustic look. Like any escabeche, this dish needs to be made several days ahead to allow time for the flavors to blend and mellow. Cook the potatoes the day you plan to serve this. I know the ingredient list is rather formidable, but once you have the components, it's not difficult at all to make this fabulous dish. Natural jute twine is available at most hardware and garden stores.

— SERVES 4

GOLDEN POTATOES

1½ pounds large yellow potatoes, peeled

2 tablespoons kosher salt

1 teaspoon turmeric

■ Using a sharp paring knife, pare the potatoes into fairly even ovals. Cut into ¾-inch slices and reserve in a bowl of cold water. Bring a large pot of water to the boil with the salt. Add the potato slices and bring back to the boil. Boil 5 minutes; then add the turmeric. Continue to boil until the potatoes are tender but still firm when pricked with a fork, about 5 minutes.

■ Place the pot of potatoes in the sink and run cold water into it to reduce the water temperature gradually. Continue to run cold water into the pot until the potatoes are cool enough to touch. Scoop the potatoes from the water and reserve. This helps keep their nice, even shape while preventing them from breaking apart.

MACKEREL ESCABECHE

4 king mackerel steaks, about ¾ pound each and 2 inches thick

2 cups plus 2 tablespoons extra virgin olive oil

Kosher salt and freshly ground black pepper to taste

1 large Spanish onion, peeled and cut into ¼-inch dice

1 tablespoon curry powder

1 tablespoon ground cumin

½ teaspoon turmeric

20 cloves garlic, peeled and thinly sliced

2 habanero chiles, cut into quarters and seeded (see Special Ingredients)

12 fresh bay leaves

¼ bunch fresh thyme (on the branch)

2 cups sherry wine vinegar

1 tablespoon dried Mexican oregano (see Special Ingredients)

1 teaspoon sugar

½ teaspoon freshly ground black pepper

¼ teaspoon ground allspice

2 whole cloves

6-inch piece canela (soft-stick cinnamon; see Special Ingredients)

1 tablespoon kosher salt

1 each red, yellow, and green bell pepper, seeded and cut into ¼-inch dice

■ Preheat a grill until red-hot. Cut 4 pieces of twine, each 2 feet in length. Wrap each length twice around a mackerel steak; then tie in the center of one side with a double knot. Rub the mackerel lightly with 2 tablespoons of the olive oil, and sprinkle on both sides with salt and pepper. Place the mackerel steaks cut-side down onto the grill diagonal to the grate. Grill 4 to 6 minutes or until well marked from the grill; then turn each mackerel steak 90 degrees and grill again. Turn over and repeat on the other side. The mackerel doesn't have to be cooked all the way through—just until firm, with prominent grill marks. Transfer to a platter and reserve.

■ To serve, divide the wakame salad between 4 small bowls. Dip one side of each fish chunk into a small bowl containing the remaining sesame seed mixture. (You won't need all the seeds, but it's easier to coat the fish if you have a little extra.) Place the fish on top of the seaweed salad and garnish each portion with a Rice Croqueta.

TOASTED BLACK AND TAN SESAME SEEDS

2 tablespoons vegetable oil
½ cup black sesame seeds
½ cup natural tan (unhulled) sesame seeds
½ teaspoon kosher salt

■ In a small skillet, heat the oil to moderately hot. Add the black and the natural sesame seeds to the pan. Toss to coat evenly with the oil; then reduce the heat to moderate and cook, shaking frequently, just until the tan seeds turn golden brown and both seeds give off a strong aroma of sesame, about 5 minutes. Remove the toasted seeds from the pan and drain on paper towels. Transfer to a small bowl and toss lightly with the salt. Store at room temperature for up to 1 week.

Chilean Sea Bass

Chilean sea bass, *Dissostichus eleginoides,* swim from the Pacific coast of Chile through the turbulent waters of the Straits of Magellan off Cape Horn, into the Atlantic near Argentina. It was much less popular when it was known as "Patagonian toothfish." Once the marketing people came up with a name Americans could associate with a fish they already loved—sea bass—its popularity exploded. However, because the demand became so fierce, the supply began to diminish. Whereas I used to get big fish that weighed about 24 pounds, lately all I've been able to buy are 12-pounders.

It's easy to see why Chilean sea bass is so popular. It has good-sized, thick, meaty fillets of white meat with a mild flavor and a pleasantly firm texture. Best of all for the kitchen, its high fat content makes it almost impossible to overcook. Chilean sea bass resembles the sablefish or "black cod" of the North Pacific. Both are predatory deepwater fish, and both are high in fat (about 16 percent), much of which is of the omega-3 unsaturated variety. Apart from a slight difference in texture—Chilean sea bass meat forms larger flakes—the two species can be used interchangeably.

Monkfish Liver Ceviche
with Haricots Verts and Meyer Lemons

Like many chefs, I've recently become enamored of the marvelous Meyer lemon. A seasonal treat from California, these lemons are named for the plant explorer Frank Meyer, who brought them back from China in 1908. Meyers have a complex, haunting flavor and their aroma hints of sweet lime, lemon, and mandarin orange. Here I use preserved Meyers, which take three weeks to cure.

The monkfish liver, a rather exotic item, actually tastes quite like foie gras. The liver is only available in the fall. If you're determined to make this dish in another season, substitute foie gras. However, when made according to the original recipe, this ceviche is a real knockout.

SERVES 4

1 fresh monkfish liver, about ½ pound

2 teaspoons ground toasted coriander seed

2 teaspoons ground toasted cumin seed

1 tablespoon kosher salt

½ teaspoon freshly ground black pepper

½ pound haricots verts, stem ends trimmed off

¼ Preserved Meyer Lemon (see recipe on page 88), soaked in cold water 20 minutes

5 tablespoons mild extra virgin olive oil

Pinch hot red pepper flakes

1 tablespoon fresh lemon juice

2 tablespoons finely minced Preserved Meyer Lemon rind

■ Clean the membrane from the exterior of the liver. Spread out the liver and turn so that the underside faces you. Pull out and discard any visible veins or connective tissue. In a shallow plate, combine the coriander, cumin, 2 teaspoons of the salt, and ¼ teaspoon of the black pepper. Roll the liver in this mixture to coat it. Wrap the liver tightly in aluminum foil, twisting the ends of the foil like candy wrappers to form a firm log shape.

■ Bring a medium saucepan of water to the boil. Place a small steamer basket over the pot. Add the liver, and cover. Reduce heat to a simmer and steam gently for 20 minutes. Remove from the heat and refrigerate, still wrapped in foil.

■ Have ready a medium bowl of water mixed with ice. Bring a medium saucepan of salted water to the boil. Add the haricots verts and bring quickly back to the boil, stirring occasionally so the beans cook evenly. Boil for 3 minutes, or until the beans are brilliant emerald green and slightly softened. Drain and plunge into the ice water. Swish around until the beans are cold and their color has set; then drain.

■ Scrape away and discard the pulp from the lemon quarter. Combine the rind, olive oil, red pepper flakes, 1 teaspoon kosher salt, ¼ teaspoon black pepper, and lemon juice in the jar of a blender. Blend until smooth and creamy, about 1 minute. Fold in the minced lemon rind.

■ Preheat a grill (preferably using hardwood charcoal) or a broiler. Cut a 1-inch slice off the top and bottom of the pineapple and stand it upright. Using a sharp knife, cut down the sides of the pineapple in long strips to remove the skin. Continue cutting until all the skin has been removed. Cut away any remaining "eyes," using the tip of a paring knife. Cut the pineapple lengthwise into ⅜-inch slabs. Discard the hard core.

■ Brush the pineapple with a little of the Pineapple–Chile Pequin Salsa and grill or broil until well browned, with crusty edges.

■ Cut the grilled pineapple into rectangles 2 inches long by 3 inches wide. Cut the unagi into pieces the same size as the pineapple. Make 2 stacks by layering 1 piece of pineapple on the bottom, topping with a layer of unagi, and then with a piece of pineapple. Repeat for a total of 4 layers of pineapple and 3 layers of unagi in each stack.

■ Secure the layers by piercing with 4 sugar cane spears, one in the center of each quadrant of the stack. Using a serrated knife, slice down the center of each stack to make 2 smaller rectangular stacks, each secured with 2 sugar cane skewers.

■ Place a stack on each of 4 serving plates. Drizzle with the remaining salsa, garnish each plate with a portion of the grilled unagi skin, and serve immediately.

Sugar Cane Skewers

I use fresh sticks of sugar cane as skewers. The heated cane releases a burst of sweet juice when bitten into. To prepare, use a heavy chef's knife or a cleaver to cut through the sugar cane, splitting it once lengthwise and then splitting each length again. Continue splitting until you obtain sticks about the size and thickness of a bamboo skewer. When buying sugar cane, choose unblemished cane; store unopened packages in a cool, dry place up to 3 months.

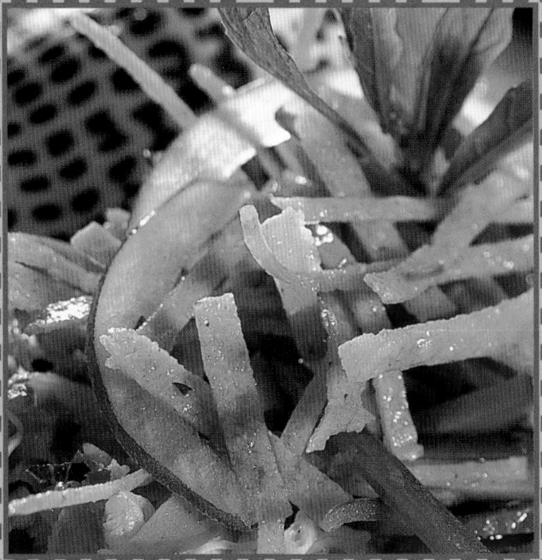

COOKED SEAFOOD
CEVICHE

Grilled Baby Octopus Ceviche,
Tomato and Cucumber Salad, Trio of Olives

Serve this dish of delectably tender baby octopus with crunchy tostones *of plantain, or* platano. *The hot, just-grilled octopus, the marinated olive strips, and the chilled cucumbers and tomatoes make a palate-pleasing combination. I like to use a mixture of large, rounded purple Alphonso and pointy purple-black Kalamata olives from Greece, along with both red and green Cerignola olives from Italy for best color and flavor contrast. The olives may be prepared up to one week ahead and are also delicious sprinkled on a green salad or used to garnish grilled or broiled fish. I garnish the salad with crumbled salty white cotija cheese, which tastes a bit like Greek feta.*

——— **SERVES 4**

MARINATED BABY OCTOPUS

3 quarts Basic Braising Liquid
    (see recipe on page 182)
12 baby octopus (26–40 count), defrosted
Juice and grated zest of 1 lemon
½ teaspoon crushed hot red
    pepper flakes
3 tablespoons extra virgin olive oil
2 tablespoons truffle oil
½ teaspoon chopped garlic
2 tablespoons chopped Italian parsley

■ In a large pot, bring the braising liquid to a boil. Add the octopus, stirring so they cook evenly. Cook 2 minutes or until the octopus is just firm to the touch. Drain; then run under cold water to cool, and reserve.

■ Whisk together the lemon juice and zest, red pepper flakes, olive oil, truffle oil, garlic, and parsley, and reserve. At least 30 minutes before serving but no more than 2 hours ahead of time, toss the poached octopus with the marinade.

TOMATO AND CUCUMBER SALAD, TRIO OF OLIVES

12 large cured olives, pitted
    (mixed varieties)
¼ red onion, peeled and thinly sliced
¼ cup balsamic vinegar
1 English cucumber, lightly peeled
    and cut into ¼-inch dice
12 each yellow and red teardrop
    tomatoes, halved lengthwise
8 Tostones de Platano (see recipe
    on page 137)
¼ cup crumbled cotija cheese
    (see Special Ingredients)

■ Using a sharp paring knife, cut the olives lengthwise into thin strips. Combine with the red onion and balsamic vinegar. Cover and marinate for at least 1 day and up to 1 week ahead of time.

■ Just before serving, preheat a grill until red-hot. Grill the octopus about 5 minutes, until the bodies are lightly charred and the tentacles curl. Toss the grilled octopus with the olive salad, cucumber, and tomatoes. Garnish with the Tostones de Platano and cotija cheese and serve immediately.

Octopus

Octopus, like squid, are cephalopods, but octopus have eight tentacles. Most weigh about 3 pounds. Here we use tender whole baby octopus that weigh only a few ounces. Fresh or frozen raw octopus is purplish or brownish gray in color but otherwise resembles the octopus as it is found alive in water. The cooked meat is firm and slightly chewy, yet tender with a mild flavor. All parts of the octopus can be eaten except the eyes, mouth area, and inner organs. The babies come frozen and already cleaned, so they are easy to use. I cook them for only a few minutes, until they are just firm and opaque.

Surf Clam Ceviche
with Mango, Banana, and Squid Ink Salad

The special Canadian surf clams I use in this dish have bright red tips. They are called hokkigai *in Japan, where they are much sought after in sushi bars and are usually very expensive. Look for frozen hokkigai in Asian markets. I happen to love them, so I created a dramatic Nuevo Latino ceviche to showcase them. The unusual black salad is both hot and sweet. I make it with mild-flavored squid ink, serrano chile, mango, and banana. The squid ink, often sold frozen, is called* ka-sumi *in Japanese.*

SERVES 4

1 serrano chile (see Special Ingredients)

2 firm but ripe mangos, peeled and pitted

1 banana, ripe but still firm, peeled

½ cup canned mango nectar

1 tablespoon fresh lime juice

2 teaspoons squid ink (see Special Ingredients)

½ teaspoon kosher salt

¼ red onion, cut into small dice

14 surf clams

■ Roast the serrano chile over an open flame until the skin is completely charred. When cool enough to handle, cut in half, discarding the seeds and stem. Cut one mango into rough chunks and reserve. To make the sauce, combine the serrano chile with the mango chunks, half the banana, mango nectar, lime juice, squid ink, and salt in a blender jar. Blend until smooth. Taste for seasoning, adding a little extra lime juice and salt if necessary.

■ Cut the remainder of the first mango into small, even dice. Cut the remainder of the banana into dice of the same size. Lightly toss the sauce with the diced mango, banana, and onion.

■ Slice each clam in half lengthwise, to make 2 thin slices. Divide the clams with points facing right in one pile and those remaining in a second pile. Thinly slice the remaining mango, and trim the slices into triangle shapes slightly larger than the clams. On each of 4 salad plates, arrange 7 matching (left- or right-handed) surf clams, all facing the same way, alternating with the mango triangles. Place a dollop of salad in the center of each plate and serve immediately.

Chef's Note: Blenders

Although many people have food processors in their kitchens, I often prefer to use a blender because I like the smoother texture it produces. Blenders have been a popular kitchen tool in Latin America for many years, and recipe books there are full of recipes that use them. I also recommend buying an inexpensive stick blender (or immersion blender) for this and other recipes. It is so easy to use and, even better, easy to clean. Mine is made by Braun, and I don't think I could cook without it.

Octopus Ceviche
with Haitian Eggplant Salad

This ceviche features a wonderful marinated eggplant salad from Haiti, topped with slow-poached octopus. To stimulate the palate with contrasting textures, I garnish it with crisp, thinly sliced Japanese eggplant chips. Both the eggplant salad and the chips are delicious on their own. Although it's not absolutely necessary, I like to add a spoonful of Japanese pickled ginger, commonly served with sushi, for a little extra flavor. For the neatest results, have ready a metal ring mold about five inches in diameter to shape the eggplant salad.

— SERVES 8

MARINATED OCTOPUS

1 large poached octopus, about 8
　　pounds (see Poached Octopus
　　on page 186)
¼ cup fresh lime juice
6 tablespoons extra virgin olive oil
1 tablespoon kosher salt
½ teaspoon freshly ground
　　black pepper
¼ cup thinly sliced scallions

■ Cut the cooled octopus body and thick portions of the tentacles into small cubes. Reserve the curled tips of the octopus tentacles for garnish. In a large nonreactive (stainless-steel or enameled) bowl, whisk together the lime juice, olive oil, salt, and pepper. Add the octopus and scallions and toss to combine. Cover and refrigerate until ready to serve, up to 1 day in advance.

ASSEMBLING THE OCTOPUS CEVICHE

2 cups Haitian Eggplant Salad
　　(see recipe on page 160)
Marinated Octopus
12 to 15 Crispy Japanese Eggplant
　　Chips (see recipe on page 147)

■ Scoop ½ cup of the Eggplant Salad into a 5-inch ring mold set in the center of each of 4 salad plates. Spread the eggplant out to the edges of the mold in a layer about ½ inch thick. Top the eggplant with one-quarter of the Marinated Octopus. To garnish, stick 4 to 5 Eggplant Chips upright into the eggplant salad, and serve immediately.

Hot Smoked Squid Ceviche
with Chayote Escabeche, Three Chile Orange Sauce

If you can buy already cleaned fresh squid from your fish market, this is an easy and fabulous dish to prepare. Because squid is rather bland, it takes well to the mixture of chiles and spices rubbed into it before hot smoking. The term "hot smoked" refers to cooking at a temperature high enough to make the smoke penetrate the food. Squid cooks very quickly and readily absorbs the smoke flavor. It is perfectly complemented by this rich, full-bodied Three Chile Orange Sauce.

SERVES 6

1 teaspoon chile ancho powder
(see Special Ingredients)
½ teaspoon chipotle powder
(see Special Ingredients)
1 teaspoon paprika
¼ teaspoon granulated garlic
¼ cup cilantro leaves
¼ cup vegetable oil
2 teaspoons kosher salt
3 pounds small, cleaned squid,
tentacles and bodies included
¼ cup Three Chile Orange Sauce
(see recipe on page 157)
¼ cup fresh lemon juice
2 tablespoons sherry vinegar
2 cups Chayote Escabeche
(see recipe on page 165)

■ Combine ancho powder, chipotle powder, paprika, garlic, cilantro, vegetable oil, and salt in a blender jar and purée, or use an immersion blender in a bowl or jar. Scrape the mixture into a large bowl and add the squid. Cover and refrigerate for about 1 hour to marinate.

■ Have ready a hot-smoking assembly following the directions in Chef's Techniques on page 14, and heat the wood chips until smoking properly.

■ Remove the squid from the refrigerator and place them on the wire rack. Close the lid of the box and smoke for 30 minutes, or until the squid are opaque and the tentacles curled and lightly browned. The smoke should never be thick and white, an indication that the temperature is too high. You should just be able to see thin strands of smoke escaping. Overly hot smoke will result in a bitter taste.

■ Lightly whisk together the Three Chile Orange Sauce, lemon juice, and sherry vinegar. Arrange alternating squid bodies and Chayote Escabeche wedges around each of 6 shallow bowls. Place the squid tentacles in the center and drizzle the sauce mixture on top. Serve immediately.

Squid

The common squid, *Loligo pealei,* is a cephalopod, like octopus. Squid have cigar-shaped bodies with two fins on either side that keep them balanced and aid in swimming. They range in size from several inches long to 56 feet, although we eat only the smaller ones that live close to shore. Squid are sold either whole or cleaned. Whole, they are covered with a thin, purplish skin, which is usually removed. Cleaned, they are bright white and firm, with their tentacles often intact and attached. Squid have firm, tender meat that turns chewy only when overcooked. Because fresh squid spoils very quickly, be especially attentive when purchasing it. Asian markets are a good place to buy it, though you probably want to have the fishmonger clean it for you. Squid that has been properly frozen will retain its flavor and texture. Defrost in the refrigerator and use within one day.

Jumbo Lump Crab Ceviche,
Tomatillo Salsa

Sweet, tender chunks of East Coast blue crab from the back leg or "backfin" section go into this light and mild ceviche. Try to wait until summer, the height of crab season, to make the dish. Crab caught in colder weather may be dredged from the ocean floor, where the crabs seek warmth. This is apt to be sandy and higher in price. I avoid pasteurized crabmeat because the high heat needed to can it destroys a lot of its delicate flavor. The cachuchas have plenty of pepper flavor without the bite of a hot chile.

SERVES 4

1 cup diced tomatillos

¼ cup diced red onion, rinsed in
  cold water and drained

2 tablespoons minced cachucha
  chiles (see Special Ingredients)

2 tablespoons fresh lime juice

1 tablespoon extra virgin olive oil

1 tablespoon chopped fresh cilantro

2 teaspoons kosher salt

½ teaspoon freshly ground
  black pepper

1 pound jumbo lump crabmeat,
  shells picked out and discarded

¼ cup vegetable oil

½ cup raw peanuts

4 Goat Cheese–Stuffed Cachucha
  Chiles (see recipe on page 143)

■ In a medium bowl, combine the tomatillos, onion, chiles, lime juice, olive oil, cilantro, salt, and pepper. Gently fold the crabmeat into the tomatillo mixture. Cover and refrigerate for up to 2 hours.

■ Heat the vegetable oil in a medium skillet over moderate heat. Add the peanuts and cook until evenly browned, shaking the pan often, for 4 minutes. Drain the peanuts through a sieve to remove excess oil. Divide the crabmeat ceviche between 4 salad plates. Sprinkle with the peanuts and top each portion with a Goat Cheese–Stuffed Cachucha Chile.

Cachucha Chiles

Also known as *rocatillos*, cachucha chiles are tiny and bonnet-shaped, resembling in appearance, but not fire, their close cousins the infamous habanero and Scotch bonnet pepper. They are only used fresh. Cachuchas are sold in Latino markets, especially those with a Puerto Rican clientele. They are crisp-textured and mildly hot, with enough pungency to be interesting.

Tomatillos

The tomatillo, also called Mexican green tomato, belongs to the same large nightshade family as the tomato. In fact, it resembles a small green tomato in size, shape, and appearance, except for its thin, parchmentlike husk. Although tomatillos can ripen to yellow, they are generally used while still green and quite firm. Their flavor has hints of lemon, apple, and herbs. Tomatillos are sometimes available in specialty produce stores, Latin American markets, and an increasing number of supermarkets. Choose firm fruit with dry, tight-fitting husks. Store in a paper bag in the refrigerator for up to a month. Remove husk and wash fruit before using.

Lobster and Vanilla Bean Ceviche,

Cara Cara Pinks

Like many chefs, I am inspired by a beautiful new fruit to create recipes such as this one, which marries tart, rosy-pink Cara Cara oranges with lobster and fragrant vanilla bean. Be sure to use a plump, aromatic vanilla bean. Sometimes the beans sit on the shelf for so long that they become dry and brittle. It's best to buy the whole beans from a specialty spice company. To accentuate the vanilla flavor, I use a touch of the Yucatecan liqueur Xtabentun, flavored with honey and vanilla. This liqueur has a reputation as an effective aphrodisiac, so if you make a trip to Cancun, bring back a bottle.

SERVES 2 AS AN APPETIZER

1 (1½-pound) half-cooked lobster
(see Cooking Lobsters on
page 186)

1 vanilla bean, halved lengthwise

½ cup fresh orange juice

2 tablespoons fresh lime juice

1 tablespoon fresh lemon juice

2 teaspoons Xtabentun liqueur
(or anisette)

1 serrano chile, seeded and minced

2 tablespoons kosher salt

2 Cara Cara pink oranges, peeled
and cut into sections with
membranes removed

6 to 8 sticks Crunchy Vanilla Beans
(see recipe on page 146)

■ Follow the directions for Cooking Lobsters, but cook only 4 minutes so that the lobster is firm enough to remove from the shells but still not completely cooked. Twist the tail and both claws off the lobster body. Remove the shell from the tail and cut the tail meat into large chunks. To crack the claws, tap them with the side of a heavy chef's knife. Remove the claw shells. Using kitchen shears, cut up the sides of the lobster "knuckle" sections and remove the meat. Cut the claw and "knuckle" meat into large chunks.

■ Scrape the tiny seeds and dark brown pulp from the vanilla bean halves. Place in a medium bowl and add the orange juice, lime juice, lemon juice, liqueur, chile, and salt. Add the lobster meat and toss to combine. Marinate in the refrigerator for 20 minutes. Divide lobster mixture between 2 medium serving bowls, alternating with sections of orange. Garnish with the Crunchy Vanilla Beans and serve immediately.

Cara Cara Pinks

The Cara Cara pink navel orange is one of a number of exotic citrus varieties that have come on the scene lately. Originally from Venezuela, Cara Cara oranges, a type of red navel now grown in the Western states, are available in November and December. You may be able to find them in specialty produce stores. They are similar to the familiar Washington navels, but the interior is dark pink to red, and the flesh is a lovely warm pink. If you can't find Cara Caras, you could substitute navel or blood oranges.

Shrimp Ceviche

in Blackened Tomato and Pepper Gazpacho

This easy ceviche is a real crowd pleaser, enjoyed even by people who are not sure they like ceviche. For perfect, chunky texture, grind the grilled vegetables with an old-fashioned meat grinder. You can also pulse them in a food processor with an on-off motion, though the texture will be different. Buy the corn nuts at natural foods stores, where they are sold near the nuts and beans, or in the supermarket snack department.

SERVES 8

4 plum tomatoes

1 red bell pepper

½ red onion with skin on

1 jalapeño chile

2 shallots, peeled

3 cloves garlic, peeled

1 cucumber, peeled and cut
   into chunks

3 tablespoons extra virgin olive oil

¼ cup tomato juice

2 tablespoons fresh lime juice

2 tablespoons fresh orange juice

1 tablespoon Crystal hot sauce
   (or other cayenne pepper sauce)

1 teaspoon ketchup

2 teaspoons kosher salt

2 pounds large shrimp (21–25 count)

1 quart Basic Braising Liquid
   (see recipe on page 182)

2 tablespoons kosher salt

1 cup corn nuts

■ Preheat a grill to very hot. Grill the tomatoes, bell pepper, onion, jalapeño, shallots, and garlic until almost entirely blackened. Remove from the grill. When vegetables are cool enough to handle, peel the red pepper, leaving the skin on the jalapeño. Halve and discard the seeds from the red pepper and jalapeño.

■ Grind the grilled tomatoes, bell pepper, onion, jalapeño, shallots, garlic, and raw cucumber in a meat grinder or food processor. If using a grinder, pour in the olive oil after grinding the vegetables, and grind again; the oil will clean the grinder of any remaining vegetable pieces. Otherwise, add the olive oil directly to the vegetable mixture. Transfer the mixture to a bowl and whisk in tomato juice, lime juice, orange juice, hot sauce, ketchup, and 2 teaspoons salt.

■ Peel the shrimp, leaving the tail sections intact, then split them halfway down the backs to devein and butterfly. Bring a medium pot of the Basic Braising Liquid to the boil with the remaining salt. Drop in the shrimp. Cook, stirring, just until opaque, about 2 minutes. Drain and rinse under cold water.

■ To serve, pour the gazpacho into 1 large or 8 individual shallow bowls. Arrange the shrimp with their butterflied tails down. Sprinkle the corn nuts in between the shrimp and serve immediately.

Rock Shrimp and Spicy Mango Ceviche,
Tasajo and Mint Salad

In this ceviche with a Brazilian theme, I use tasajo, *or dried beef, as a seasoning condiment. Strong and salty, it contrasts beautifully with the mild rock shrimp and spicy mango. The powerful, cleansing flavor of fresh mint brings the whole dish to life. The African bird pepper, also known as* malagueta *pepper, I use here is shaped like a bird's beak. This small, red, extremely hot chile with fruity overtones must be handled with care.*

SERVES 4

4 ounces tasajo (see Special Ingredients)

1 quart Basic Braising Liquid (see recipe on page 182)

2 teaspoons kosher salt

1 pound rock shrimp

1 firm, ripe mango

½ cup fresh lime juice

1 African bird pepper, seeded and sliced into paper-thin rings (see Special Ingredients) (substitute serrano chile)

1 tablespoon mild olive oil

½ teaspoon freshly ground black pepper

2 tablespoons chiffonade of fresh mint, preferably spearmint

■ Simmer the tasajo for 1 hour in water to cover, drain, and then repeat twice more, or until the tasajo is tender enough to pull apart. Drain; then shred the meat and reserve.

■ In a medium pot, bring the Basic Braising Liquid and 1 teaspoon salt to the boil. Drop the rock shrimp into the pot and stir so that the shrimp cook evenly. After 35 seconds, pour the shrimp into a colander and rinse with cold water to stop the cooking.

■ Peel the mango and cut into ½-inch cubes. In a medium nonreactive (stainless-steel or enameled) bowl, combine the shrimp, mango, half the lime juice, bird pepper rings, and ½ teaspoon salt.

■ In a separate bowl, combine the shredded tasajo with the remaining lime juice, olive oil, remaining ½ teaspoon salt, pepper, and mint.

■ To serve, arrange the Rock Shrimp and Spicy Mango Ceviche in a ring around the outside of a platter. Place the tasajo mixture in the center and serve immediately.

Tasajo

Tasajo, a dried, salt-cured beef much like beef jerky, was originally the food of slaves. Also known as *carne seca*, it is popular in Latin American cooking, particularly in Cuba, Brazil, and my native Argentina. Buy tasajo in Hispanic markets. The Cajun and Creole tasso ham—smoked and seasoned with cayenne pepper, garlic, and salt—is related to tasajo, though it is made with pork instead of beef. Dried beef (or chipped beef) can be used as a substitute.

Rock Shrimp

The rock shrimp, *Sicyonia brevirostris*, is a deep-water cousin of pink, brown, and white shrimp. Its hard shell is similar to that of other deep-water crustaceans like lobster. Look for rock shrimp with transparent or clear white flesh and a mild, oceanic smell. They are sold already peeled and cleaned, making them a cinch to cook. Because of their small size, they cook very quickly.

Panamanian White Shrimp Ceviche
with Jicama and Thai Basil Slaw

Here I use the mild-flavored, large white shrimp that are a specialty of Panama. These tropical shrimp, Penaeus vannamei, are flown in during their short season from April through the end of summer. Substitute the largest, freshest whole shrimp you can find. I make a crunchy sweet-and-savory slaw with jicama and Thai basil to accompany the shrimp and flavor it with chile de arbol. This chile gets its name from the Spanish word for a small tree, which is exactly what these slim, tapered chiles resemble. In Mexico they're also called "bird's beak" or "rat's tail." Small and extremely hot, they are used both fresh and dried. I serve this ceviche in a young coconut shell, but as they're tricky to cut, you might not want to attempt it.

SERVES 4

1 pound large Panamanian white
   shrimp, heads on
¾ cup fresh lime juice
4 teaspoons kosher salt
1 jicama root, peeled
¼ cup mild olive oil
½ cup Thai basil leaves
½ chile de arbol, seeded (see
   Special Ingredients)
Pinch black pepper
1 whole chile de arbol, for garnish
1 whole sprig Thai basil, blossoming
   if possible

■ Peel the shells from the bodies of the shrimp, leaving their heads and the last segment of tail shells intact. In a large bowl, mix the lime juice with 1 tablespoon of salt. Add the shrimp and toss to combine. Cover and refrigerate for 2 hours to lightly cure.

■ Using a mandoline or Benriner cutter, cut the jicama into matchsticks. In a blender or food processor, purée the oil, basil, chile de arbol, pepper, and remaining salt. Scrape the sauce into a large bowl and add the jicama. Mix well to combine.

■ To serve, arrange the shrimp on a large platter. Place the jicama slaw in the center and serve immediately, garnished with the whole chile and basil if desired.

Jicama

Surprisingly, jicama, or Mexican yam bean, is actually the root of a plant in the legume (bean) family. Native to Mexico and South America, it is sold as a street food there, peeled and cut into pieces with a squeeze of lime and a shake of fiery chili powder. Jicama is available in two varieties: *agua* (watery juice) and *leche* (milky juice). One jicama can weigh up to 6 pounds. Its crisp, white flesh is hidden under a fibrous brown skin, which must be completely peeled or simply pulled off. Jicama is equally delicious when served cooked (resembling water chestnuts in texture) or raw, as in this sweet, crunchy slaw.

Sea Urchin and Stone Crab Ceviche,
Russian Salad

In summertime in Buenos Aires, my mother would serve us large, hollowed-out tomatoes filled with this Russian salad and topped with fresh poached fish or shellfish. Here I've used the same idea, making a Russian salad of very small balls of vegetables dressed with a fresh lime mayonnaise, topped with stone crab salad and delectable sea urchin roe. Sea urchins resemble small, round porcupines with their dark purple spines. Their roe is a delicacy that has long been popular in France but is just beginning to be discovered in this country.

SERVES 4

SEA URCHIN AND STONE CRAB CEVICHE

4 live sea urchins, soaked in cold water for about 30 minutes, until the water looks clean

2 teaspoons fresh lime juice

4 whole fresh stone crab claws

¼ cup Lime Allioli (see recipe on page 156)

Kosher salt and freshly ground black pepper to taste

■ Cut open each sea urchin (see box). Carefully remove the roe, and place it in a small bowl of ice water for about 15 minutes. This will firm up the roe. Drain the shells and place them in a pot of boiling water for about 1 minute to brighten the color; then drain and toss with lime juice. Refrigerate until ready to serve, up to 1 hour.

■ To prepare the stone crab claws, twist off the "knuckle" or upper portion of the claw. Use heavy-duty kitchen shears to cut along one side of the shell, and discard the shell. Use this meat to make the salad. Use the back of a spoon to lightly tap the plumpest part of the claw shell. Continue tapping until you can remove the top half of the shell all around the claw. The meat should then be exposed, held in place in a collar of shell. Rinse lightly to remove any shell bits. Cover and refrigerate until ready to serve.

■ In a small bowl, combine the crab knuckle meat, Lime Allioli, salt, and pepper. Cover and refrigerate until ready to serve.

Cutting Sea Urchins

It's best to wear heavy gardening gloves to protect yourself from the sharp spines when working with sea urchins. Before proceeding with a recipe, soak the urchins in a sinkful of cold water for about 30 minutes, changing the water several times until it's clear. To prepare, hold each urchin with the "mouth" (the small, round opening in the center) facing you. Using a pair of heavy shears, make a cut near the soft part around the mouth. Cut toward the outside about 1 inch from the edge; then cut around in a circle. Remove and discard the cut circle of shell, the attached innards, and any dark innards inside the shell. Rinse under cold running water until all that's left inside are the bright orange sections of tongue-shaped roe. This is the only edible part of the sea urchin.

RUSSIAN SALAD

2 large carrots, peeled

2 large yellow potatoes, peeled

2 large purple potatoes, peeled

1 cup trimmed and cut green beans in ¼-inch lengths

1 cup fresh shelled green peas

6 tablespoons Lime Allioli (see recipe page 156)

Kosher salt and freshly ground black pepper to taste

■ Use a small melon baller to scoop evenly sized balls from the vegetables, or cut each vegetable into small dice. Bring a medium saucepan of heavily salted water to the boil. Keep the water at a rolling boil, and in the order listed, one at a time, cook each vegetable for about 2 minutes, or until brightly colored and tender but not mushy. As each vegetable is cooked, scoop it from the water, using a wire skimmer or slotted spoon. Rinse under cold water to set the color and stop the cooking; then drain. Just before serving, combine the vegetables with 4 tablespoons of the Lime Allioli. Season to taste with salt and pepper.

■ To serve, place each sea urchin shell on a medium plate and divide most of the Russian Salad between the shells. Top with one-quarter of the crab claw salad and arrange the drained roe on top. Garnish each serving with a stone crab claw. Spoon the remaining Russian salad onto each plate and drizzle attractively with the remaining 2 tablespoons of Lime Allioli. Serve immediately.

Stone Crabs

Stone crabs, *Menippe mercenaria*, have dramatically colored, extremely hard-shelled claws and are high on the list of favored Florida seafoods. They are called *merceneria* because of the high commercial or "mercenary" value of their claws. Stone crabs have two large, meat-filled claws of unequal size that are highly desired by seafood lovers. The claws are the only edible part of this crab; in fact, by law only one claw at a time may be removed from the crab. The crab must then be dropped back into the water to give it a chance to grow another claw. The tips of the claws are black, with creamy white shells tinted with orange. Common throughout the Gulf of Mexico, stone crabs are found from North Carolina to Cuba, the Bahamas, and Mexico, though most of our commercial catch comes from Florida.

Conch and Peekytoe Crab Ceviche,
Green Olive and Crispy Tortilla Salad

For this dish, I buy white conch meat already extracted from the shell and frozen. To make the crab salad, I use Jonah crab, commonly known as "peekytoe crab." Its sweet and subtle flavor has made it a favorite among chefs around the country, myself included. Like many chefs, I am also a fan of grapeseed oil. In fact, I use it twice in this recipe. Because of its stability and extremely high smoking point, grapeseed oil is ideal for deep-frying. I also use it in the ceviche dressing because its mild, clean flavor won't overwhelm the delicate taste of the crab. I garnish the salad with sprouts of epazote, the pungent herb sometimes known as Mexican wormweed. This is a relatively new product that I get from a specialty grower. You can easily substitute spicy radish sprouts.

SERVES 4

½ pound white conch meat, defrosted if frozen

½ cup fresh lime juice

1 tablespoon kosher salt

6 to 8 large cured green olives, preferably green Cerignola, pitted

1 Maya sweet onion (or other sweet onion such as Vidalia or Texas Sweet 100s)

½ pound peekytoe crabmeat

1 red jalapeño chile, seeded and finely minced

3¼ cups grapeseed oil

2 tablespoons chiffonade of fresh cilantro

4 corn tortillas, 2 blue corn and 2 yellow corn, if possible

1 pint epazote sprouts (or radish sprouts)

■ Cut the conch into thin slices and arrange in a single layer on a platter. In a small bowl, whisk together ¼ cup of lime juice and 1 teaspoon of salt. Rub lightly into the conch, cover, and refrigerate for 2 hours to cure.

■ Slice the olives into thin julienne strips. Slice the onion into thin strips and rinse under cold water. Lightly toss together the crabmeat, olives, and onion.

■ In a small bowl, whisk together the remaining lime juice, 1½ teaspoons of salt, most of the minced red jalapeño, ¼ cup of the grapeseed oil, and the cilantro. Lightly toss half the dressing with the crabmeat mixture, reserving the remainder. Cover and refrigerate the crabmeat until ready to serve.

Conch

The giant sea snail, *Strombus gigas*, or queen conch, lives in shallow water inside a large, cone-shaped spiral shell. Conches grow up to 1 foot in length. If you've traveled in Florida, you've probably seen the shells with their huge, flaring, rose-colored lips, either in the water or for sale along the roadside. Key West, Florida, is officially named "The Conch Republic" in honor of this creature of the sea. Conch is prepared in many ways in Florida, the Bahamas, and the Cayman Islands. In some places, natives consider it to be a natural aphrodisiac.

■ Slice the tortillas into thin strips. Heat the remaining 3 cups of grapeseed oil in a wok or frying pot until it shimmers, or until it reads 375°F on a deep-fry thermometer. Add the tortilla strips and fry until crisp and just starting to color, stirring to keep the strips separate and to cook them evenly. Remove from the oil using a slotted spoon or a wire skimmer, and drain on paper towels.

■ When ready to serve, arrange the conch in a single layer in each of 4 serving plates. Sprinkle with remaining salt and pepper. Have ready a ring mold about 3 inches in diameter (or a clean empty tuna can with both ends cut off and discarded). Fill with one-quarter of the crab salad and pat down firmly to shape evenly. Remove the mold and repeat with the other plates.

■ At the last minute, lightly toss the crisp tortilla strips with half the remaining dressing. Arrange a small bundle of strips on top of each portion of crab salad. Sprinkle each portion with the epazote sprouts, drizzle the remaining dressing around the plates, and serve immediately.

Peekytoe Crab

Peekytoe or Jonah crabs, *Cancer borealis*, are harvested in the cold, clean waters off the coast of Maine, where they are steamed and picked, and their meat packed by hand. Peekytoe crab is available in specialty fish markets in large cities. If you live near the East Coast, you could substitute blue crab; on the West Coast, choose Dungeness crab. Though each type of crab has a slightly different flavor and texture, each would be delicious here.

Octopus Ceviche,

Boniato and Sweet Potato Salad

Here I combine chunks of poached, marinated octopus with chunks of roasted boniato, a tuber similar to sweet potato. I do love cooking and eating octopus. If you're new to it, don't be squeamish. Octopus is mild and tender when cooked properly, and extremely high in protein. Ask your fishmonger to clean it for you. If you can't find it in your local market, try an Asian market. Frozen octopus will work well for this dish, as long as it is cooked gently after it has been defrosted.

— SERVES 8

OCTOPUS CEVICHE

1 large poached octopus, about 8
    pounds (see instructions on
    page 186)
¼ cup fresh lemon juice
6 tablespoons extra virgin olive oil
1 tablespoon kosher salt
½ teaspoon freshly ground
    black pepper
¼ cup thinly sliced scallions

■ Thinly slice the cooled octopus body and thick portions of the tentacles. Reserve the curled tips of the octopus tentacles for garnish. In a large nonreactive (stainless-steel or enameled) bowl, whisk together the lemon juice, olive oil, salt, and pepper. Add the octopus and scallions and toss to combine. Cover and refrigerate until ready to serve, up to 1 day in advance.

BONIATO AND SWEET POTATO SALAD

2 boniatos, peeled
2 sweet potatoes, peeled
1 cup strong-flavored extra virgin
    olive oil
3 teaspoons kosher salt
½ teaspoon freshly ground
    black pepper
¼ cup distilled white vinegar
Several drops Tabasco sauce
½ large red onion, peeled and cut
    into julienne strips
2 tablespoons chopped
    Italian parsley

■ Preheat the oven to 400°F. Cut the boniatos and sweet potatoes into ¾-inch cubes. Toss with 2 tablespoons of the olive oil and half the salt and pepper. Spread the cubes in a single layer in a baking pan. Roast for 15 minutes, or until brown on the outside but still firm inside. Remove from the oven and cool.

■ In a medium bowl, combine the remaining olive oil with the vinegar, Tabasco, and remaining salt and pepper. Toss with the roasted boniatos and sweet potatoes, and add the red onion and parsley. To serve, arrange a mound of the salad in the center of each of 8 salad plates. Surround the salad with the marinated octopus and serve immediately.

Bahian Lobster Ceviche with Grilled Papaya Salad,
Passion Fruit Mojo

Bahia is the province of Brazil most influenced by Africa. It is renowned for its imaginative cooking, which evolved from plantation cooks improvising on African, Amazonian, and traditional Portuguese dishes using locally available ingredients. Seafood like the Bahian spiny lobster and tropical fruits like passion fruit and papaya are menu staples.

In Brazil, for this dish they would use clawless spiny lobsters, which populate the warmer waters of the Caribbean and the South Atlantic. I use a 1½-pound lobster, which I normally cook for seven minutes. Here I cook it only four minutes, because I want the partially cooked meat to marinate in the passion fruit mojo.

SERVES 4

2 firm but ripe papayas

2 teaspoons kosher salt

½ teaspoon freshly ground
black pepper

¼ cup olive oil

2 (1½-pound) cooked Maine lobsters
(see instructions on page 186)

½ cup passion fruit purée
(see Special Ingredients)

2 tablespoons chopped garlic

■ Preheat a grill until white-hot. Halve the papayas; then dig out and discard the seeds. Cut each half into 3 wedges. Trim off the ends and pare off a thin strip along the length of both sides of the papaya wedge. There should be no skin along the edges, only on the bottom of each wedge.

■ Sprinkle the papaya wedges with 1 teaspoon of the salt and the pepper and rub lightly with 2 tablespoons of the oil. Grill by placing the cut edges against the grill, gradually turning 90 degrees to form crosshatched grill marks, and reserve. Cut away the skin of the papaya and cut each wedge into 3 to 4 sections.

■ Pull the claws off the body of each lobster; then twist and pull off the tail portion. Cut the tail section, with the shell on, into 1-inch rings. Divide the claw from the "knuckle." Reserve the

knuckle section for another use. Crack the claws by tapping them gently with the side of a heavy chef's knife. Remove the bottom half of the claw shells. (The pointy pincer claw has a thinner, easier-to-crack shell. The larger rounded masher claw has a very thick shell.)

■ Arrange the lobsters on 2 oval platters, placing them to resemble a whole lobster with the head section at one end and the claws alongside. Arrange the cut medallions of lobster in order from the top end to the tail shell. Place the papaya chunks along either side of the lobster.

■ In a small bowl, whisk together the passion fruit purée, remaining olive oil, garlic, and remaining salt. Drizzle the mixture over the lobster and papaya, and serve immediately.

Mussel and Clam Ceviche
with Garlic, Carrot, and Pearl Onion Escabeche

This ceviche calls for several different escabeche components, each of which is delicious on its own and can also be incorporated into a variety of dishes. The mussels and clams, Garlic Escabeche, Red Pearl Onion Escabeche, and Carrot Escabeche take about 2 weeks to cure, and keep well for at least 1 month. In fact, this recipe is a good example of pantry cooking, for with a little forethought, you need only combine the ingredients and serve. It's a great idea for an outdoor summertime buffet: cool, refreshing, and ready when you are. Serve this ceviche with toasted country bread to mop up the delicious juices.

SERVES 12

MUSSEL CEVICHE

4 pounds farm-raised mussels,
    scrubbed clean
¾ cup fresh lime juice
½ cup fresh lemon juice
1½ cups extra virgin olive oil
1 tablespoon mirasol chile flakes
    (see Special Ingredients)
2 tablespoons kosher salt

■ Sort through the mussels, discarding any that are broken or not tightly closed. If a mussel is just slightly open, try pressing the edges of its shell together. If a mussel closes up, it is alive and healthy. Discard any mussels that either gape open or contain sand. Scrub, using a brush, under cold running water.

■ Place the mussels in a large pot (with a lid) with about 1 inch of water. Cover, turn the heat to high, and steam the mussels, shaking occasionally, until almost all have opened completely. They should still be plump; overcooked mussels will start to shrivel. It's better to hand-open the last few mussels all the way, rather than overcook them.

■ Remove from the heat, drain, and immediately plunge the mussels into a large bowl of ice mixed with water. Remove the mussels from their shells, using a single shell as a scraper to dislodge the mussel attached to the shell wall.

■ Sterilize a quart jar according to the directions on page 124. In a large non-reactive (stainless-steel or enameled) bowl, combine the lime juice, lemon juice, olive oil, chile flakes, and salt. Add the mussels and toss to combine. Transfer the mixture to the sterilized jar. Cover and refrigerate for at least 2 weeks, turning the jar over every few days. The pickled mussels keep well in the refrigerator for a month.

CLAM CEVICHE

6 dozen littleneck clams, scrubbed
  and soaked in cold water until
  completely free of sand
¾ cup fresh lime juice
½ cup fresh lemon juice
1½ cups extra virgin olive oil
2 tablespoons kosher salt
½ teaspoon freshly ground
  black pepper

■ Place the clams in a large pot
(with a lid) with about 1 inch of water.
Cover, turn the heat to high, and
steam the clams, shaking occasionally,
until almost all have opened completely. They should still be plump; overcooked clams will start to shrivel.
It's better to hand-open the last few
clams all the way, rather than overcook them.

■ Remove from the heat, drain, and
immediately plunge the clams into a
large bowl of ice mixed with water.
Remove the clams from their shells,
using a single shell as a scraper to
dislodge the clam attached to the
shell wall.

■ Sterilize a quart jar according to the
directions at right. In a large nonreactive (stainless-steel or enameled)
bowl, combine the lime juice, lemon
juice, olive oil, salt, and pepper. Add
the clams and toss to combine.
Transfer the mixture to the sterilized

jar. Cover and refrigerate for at least 2
weeks, turning the jar over every few
days. The pickled clams keep well in
the refrigerator for a month.

ASSEMBLING THE MUSSEL AND CLAM CEVICHE

1 cup Carrot Escabeche
  (see recipe on page 162)
½ cup Garlic Escabeche
  (see recipe on page 164)
1 cup thinly sliced scallions
1½ cups Red Pearl Onion Escabeche
  (see recipe on page 161)
½ cup chiffonade of Italian parsley
Kosher salt and freshly ground black
  pepper to taste

■ Drain the Carrot Escabeche and cut
into 1-inch lengths. Drain the Garlic
Escabeche. Drain the Mussel Ceviche,
reserving the liquid for storing any
leftovers. In a medium nonreactive
bowl, combine the carrots, garlic, and
scallions with the pickled mussels.
Taste and adjust seasoning with salt
and pepper if necessary.

■ Drain the Red Pearl Onion
Escabeche. Drain the pickled clams,
reserving the liquid for storing any
leftovers. In another medium nonreactive (stainless-steel or enameled)
bowl, combine the onions and parsley
with the pickled clams. Taste and
adjust seasoning with salt and pepper
if necessary.

■ Cover and refrigerate for up to 2
hours before serving. To serve, place
the mussel ceviche in a serving bowl
and the clam ceviche in a second bowl,
and allow guests to serve themselves.

To Sterilize Jars for Escabeche

Bring a large pot of water to the boil.
Submerge glass or clear plastic jars,
preferably tall and thin in shape, in the
water to sterilize them. Using tongs,
remove the jars from the water and
turn them upside down onto paper
towels to drain. Using the same
method, sterilize and drain the lids.
Without touching the insides of the
jars, turn them over and fill when
ready with escabeche mixture.

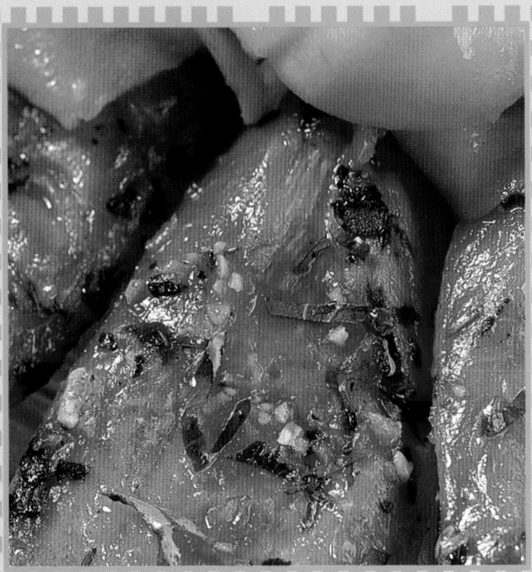

OTHER CEVICHE

Argentinean Beef Roll Ceviche

Argentina is world famous for the quality of its beef. Grass-fed rather than corn-fed like American beef, it is leaner and has a stronger, more distinctive flavor. I import Argentinean beef to serve at ¡Pasion!, where we prepare it on individual cow-shaped grills that we bring to the table. Here I've used the beef in a ceviche inspired by the Vietnamese style of raw beef salad flavored with fish sauce.

SERVES 8

MARINATED BEEF

1½ cups rice wine vinegar

½ teaspoon cayenne

¼ cup molasses

2 whole star anise

1½ teaspoons whole white
   peppercorns

1½ teaspoons mirasol chile flakes
   (see Special Ingredients)

1 teaspoon kosher salt

2 tablespoons soy sauce

2 tablespoons Thai or Vietnamese
   fish sauce (Squid brand preferred)

2 tablespoons fresh lime juice

2 teaspoons Japanese roasted
   sesame oil

½ teaspoon annatto powder or 1½
   teaspoons whole annatto seeds
   (see Special Ingredients)

1½ pounds boneless sirloin

■ In a large, nonreactive (stainless-steel or enameled) pot, combine all the ingredients except the beef. Heat gently to 108°F, just hot to the touch, to steep and blend the flavors. Cool to room temperature, cover, and refrigerate.

■ Trim the beef of all exterior fat and connective tissue, or have your butcher do this step. Place the beef in a large nonreactive container and pour in the chilled liquid. Cover and refrigerate for 24 hours to cure.

BEEF ROLLS

Marinated Beef

1 large head (or 2 small heads)
   Boston lettuce, leaves separated

1 tablespoon honey

2 tablespoons fresh lime juice

Pinch ground white pepper

■ When ready to serve, remove the beef from the marinade. Wrap in plastic wrap and freeze for 30 minutes. Remove the beef from the freezer, unwrap, and slice paper-thin. (If you have access to a deli slicer, it is ideal for this task. Otherwise, use a very sharp slicing knife.)

■ Place 1 slice of beef at a time on a work surface, and cover with 1 lettuce leaf. Loosely roll up the beef and arrange on a serving platter (rectangular if possible) in rows. Whisk together the honey, lime juice, and pepper, and drizzle over the rolls. Serve immediately.

Molasses

The purest, amber-colored molasses is made from unprocessed cane juice. To produce sugar, cane juice is first transformed into raw sugar. After this raw sugar is crystallized into refined sugar, the remaining syrup is called first molasses, the kind you want to use. The leftover syrup from the second boiling is the darker and stronger second molasses, and so on until you get blackstrap molasses, which is almost black and quite bitter. Molasses was the major sweetener used in America until after World War I, because it was less expensive than sugar. Look for molasses (Grandma's is an excellent and commonly available brand) in supermarkets and natural foods stores.

Grilled Papaya
and Pickled Green Mango Ceviche

This is an all-fruit ceviche, made from grilled papaya marinated in a ceviche mixture and served with pickled green mangos. Look for the superb Mariposa (butterfly) papayas that come from Puerto Rico in January. The large, brilliantly red papayas from Hawaii are also an excellent choice. If your papayas are not ripe enough, put them into a paper bag with a ripe peach or banana, which give off gases that will speed ripening. The incomparable habanero chile I use here and in many other ceviches is my chile of choice for salsas.

SERVES 4

2 ripe but firm papayas
Kosher salt and freshly ground
    black pepper to taste
2 tablespoons vegetable oil
¼ cup fresh lime juice
1 teaspoon kosher salt
1 teaspoon chopped garlic
1 tablespoon chopped fresh cilantro
½ cup Green Mango Escabeche
    (see recipe on page 162)

■ Preheat a grill until white-hot. Halve the papayas; then dig out and discard the seeds. Cut each half into 3 wedges. Trim off the ends and pare off a thin strip along the length of both sides of the papaya wedge. There should be no skin along the edges, only on the bottom of each wedge.

■ Sprinkle the papaya wedges with salt and pepper and rub lightly with the oil. Grill by placing the cut edges against the grill, gradually turning 90 degrees to form crosshatched grill marks.

■ To serve, arrange 3 grilled papaya wedges on each of 4 salad plates. Whisk together the lime juice, salt, garlic, and cilantro, and drizzle over the papaya. Place a small mound of Green Mango Escabeche in the center of each plate and serve immediately.

Habanero Chiles

Though fiery hot—200,000 to 300,000 Scoville units (the standard measure for hotness), as compared to jalapeños at only 2,500 to 10,000 Scoville units—habaneros have a flowery taste and aroma that create intense, distinctive sauces. A little goes a long, long way. Normally you won't need more than a half to one whole habanero in a dish. Take care to cut them with the skin side up, so that less of the incendiary chile oil gets on your fingers. You may want to wear gloves. Other names for habanero are goat pepper (in Jamaica) and Scotch bonnet (because of its shape, resembling a Scotch tam o'shanter).

Trio of Mushrooms Ceviche
with Fried Yuca Spears

Strictly speaking, this is actually an escabeche of mushrooms, because they are first cooked and then pickled in a spiced liquid. I make the mushrooms in a large quantity because they keep quite well and only taste better as they age. Be sure to use a stainless-steel spoon to remove them from the jar. Using your hands would introduce bacteria, making the mushrooms prone to spoilage.

SERVES 24

MUSHROOM CEVICHE

2 pounds small white button
    mushrooms
1 pound cremini mushrooms
½ pound fresh shiitake mushrooms
1 red onion, peeled and cut into
    thin strips
½ cup fresh orange juice
2 tablespoons fresh lime juice
¼ cup red wine vinegar
¼ cup balsamic vinegar
½ cup extra virgin olive oil
½ cup kosher salt
2 tablespoons sugar
2 tablespoons mirasol chile flakes
    (see Special Ingredients)
1 tablespoon chopped garlic
½ cup chiffonade of Italian parsley
6 cups Fried Yuca Spears
    (see recipe on page 145)

■ Clean the button and cremini mushrooms by washing in a large bowl of water, swishing around to remove any sand. Scoop from the water and drain well; then dry on paper towels. (Normally the shiitakes are already clean and don't need washing.) Using a sharp paring knife, trim off the stems of the mushrooms flush with the bottoms of the caps. Reserve the stems for another use (for example, freeze to add to a soup stock). Leave the button mushrooms whole. Slice the cremini into thin rounds. Cut the shiitake caps into ¼-inch-thick matchsticks.

■ Preheat a grill to moderate and place a wire rack, such as a cake cooling rack, on top. Arrange the mushrooms in a single layer on the rack, working in batches if necessary. Grill over moderate heat, turning the mushrooms with tongs, until evenly browned on both sides.

■ In a medium nonreactive (stainless-steel or enameled) bowl, combine the onion, orange juice, lime juice, red wine vinegar, balsamic vinegar, olive oil, salt, sugar, chile flakes, and garlic. Whisk to combine, making sure the sugar and salt are completely dissolved. Have ready several large glass or clear plastic sterilized jars (see instructions on page 124). Without touching the insides of the jars with your fingers, fill them completely with the mushroom mixture. Screw on the lids and refrigerate, leaving the mushrooms to marinate at least 2 days before using. The mushrooms will keep well for 1 month, as long as you use a stainless-steel spoon to remove them.

■ When ready to serve, drain the mushrooms, stir in the parsley, and serve with Fried Yuca Spears.

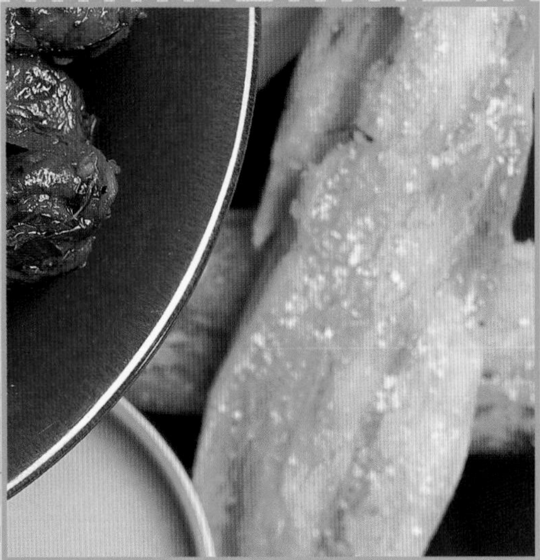

CHIPS, CROQUETAS, AND OTHER CRUNCHY THINGS

Platano Chips

Green or unripe plantains, pintos *(half-ripe plantains),* and maduros *(ripe yellow plantains with black spots) are so completely different in taste and texture that it's hard to believe they're all the same fruit at different stages. Here, starchy green plantains are cut lengthwise and fried until crispy, like the best potato chip you ever tasted. The chips will keep well for 1 day, but after that they begin to get stale.*

SERVES 8 AS A SNACK

4 green plantains
1 quart pure peanut oil, for frying
Kosher salt

■ Cut the ends off the plantains and slice down the sides, being careful to cut only through the skin and not into the flesh. Fill a large bowl with hot tap water. Soak the plantains for 30 minutes to soften them slightly. Using a spoon, carefully separate the skin from the flesh. Discard the skin, dropping the plantains back into the water until ready to cook. In a deep, heavy frying pot or Dutch oven, heat the oil to 375°F on a deep-fry thermometer.

■ Using a mandoline or Benriner slicer if possible, cut the plantains lengthwise into long, even slices about ⅛-inch thick. As soon as the plantains have been sliced, start laying one slice at a time into the hot oil. Stir before adding the next slice so they don't stick together. You will have to fry in several batches. It's important for the plantains to have enough room so you can move them around to fry evenly. Fry until golden brown on all sides, about 8 minutes. Drain on paper towels and repeat until all the plantains have been fried. Sprinkle with kosher salt and serve.

Crunchy Shallots

These shallots keep their crunch for several days and are delicious sprinkled on vegetables or fish or used as part of a ceviche. Try them on a salad or a baked potato.

SERVES 8 AS A GARNISH

2 cups unbleached flour
3 tablespoons sweet Spanish paprika
2 tablespoons kosher salt
1 tablespoon ground cumin
1 tablespoon granulated garlic
2 teaspoons cayenne
2 cups pure peanut oil, for frying
½ cup peeled shallots, cut into thin rings

■ In a large bowl, combine the flour, paprika, salt, cumin, garlic, and cayenne. In a medium-heavy frying pot or Dutch oven, heat the oil to 375°F on a deep-fry thermometer. Briefly dip the shallot rings into a bowl of cold water to wet them. Drain and toss with the flour. Remove from the flour, shaking off excess through a sieve or with your fingers. Only the flour clinging to the shallots should remain.

■ Drop the floured shallots into the hot oil a few at a time, so that they don't stick together. Fry for about 3 minutes, or until crisp and reddish-brown. Skim from the oil and drain on paper towels. Store at room temperature in a tightly sealed container.

Tostones de Platano

Here, unripe plantains are first boiled in oil to soften them, then soaked in garlic-flavored water for 24 hours to impart a unique flavor. I then flatten them and cook them a second time until browned and crisp. In South America, many cooks use a tostonero, *similar to a tortilla press, to flatten the plantains. You can buy an inexpensive tostonero at a Hispanic market, or flatten the sliced plantains with the cupped palm of your hand.*

SERVES 8 AS A SNACK

4 green plantains
4 cups pure peanut oil
1 tablespoon granulated garlic
Kosher salt

■ Cut the tips off the plantains and slice down the sides, being careful to cut only through the skin and not into the flesh. Fill a large bowl with hot tap water. Soak the plantains for 30 minutes to soften them slightly. Using a spoon, carefully separate the skin from the flesh. Discard the skin.

■ In a deep, heavy frying pot or Dutch oven, heat the oil to 250°F on a deep-fry thermometer. Cut the plantains into 2-inch lengths. Add the plantain sections to the hot oil and cook for 10 to 15 minutes, or until completely tender when pierced. Scoop the plantains from the oil and drain, reserving the oil in the pot.

■ Using a tostonero or the cupped palm of your hand, flatten the plantain slices to between ¼- and ½-inch thick. They should resemble flowers, with a banana-shaped ring in the center surrounded by the flattened flesh. (If the plantains split more than a little bit around the edges when they are flattened, they were not cooked long enough in the oil.) Chill the flattened tostones by plunging them into a large bowl filled with ice and water.

■ Transfer the cold tostones to a bowl of cold water mixed with the granulated garlic. Refrigerate for at least 1 hour and up to 24 hours in the garlic water. Reheat the oil to 375°F on a deep-fry thermometer. Fry the tostones until crisp and browned, about 4 minutes, turning so that they cook on both sides. Drain thoroughly by laying them out on paper towels. Sprinkle with kosher salt, and serve immediately.

Crispy Malanga Chips

With its wrinkled and stringy exterior, taro root (also known as malanga*) looks something like a section of an elephant's trunk. The roots can weigh as much as five pounds. When you pare away the tough outer skin, inside is bright white flesh intermingled with strands of lavender-colored fiber.*

SERVES 8 AS A SNACK

2 pounds firm taro root with no soft spots
1 quart pure peanut oil, for frying
Kosher salt

■ Have ready a large bowl of cold water. Trim off about ½ inch from the ends of the taro root. Using a sharp knife, pare the taro until only white flesh shows. Using a mandoline or Benriner cutter, slice the taro into chips about the thickness of a thick potato chip. Drop the cut chips into the cold water, leaving them there until all the chips have been cut.

■ In a deep, heavy frying pot or Dutch oven, heat the oil to 375°F on a deep-fry thermometer. The oil should come no more than a third of the way up the sides of the pan. Drain the taro chips very well in a colander, and spread out on cloth or paper towels to dry further. Add enough taro chips to the hot oil so that the surface of the oil is only half covered. Fry about 6 minutes, or until crisp but not browned, turning so they cook on both sides.

■ Scoop the taro rounds from the oil using a skimmer or slotted spoon and drain on paper towels. While still hot, sprinkle with kosher salt. Repeat the process until all the taro is cooked. Store for several days in a tightly sealed container.

Crunchy Fried Cancha

Cancha is a Peruvian specialty of large, starchy field corn kernels that have been dried. To prepare, cancha is first soaked to reconstitute it, then boiled for several hours until tender, and drained. The final step is to fry the kernels until crunchy, sprinkling them just after frying with a generous quantity of kosher salt. The process takes time, but the kernels keep well for one month in a closed container. Salty fried cancha makes an irresistible accompaniment for cocktails such as Papi Sours, which is why it's such a great bar snack. For a variation, sprinkle the fried cancha with a little Jamaican curry powder.

MAKES 4 CUPS

1 pound dried Peruvian cancha corn
  (see Special Ingredients)
1 quart pure peanut oil, for frying
Kosher salt

■ Soak the cancha in cold water to cover by several inches overnight or for at least 8 hours. Drain and rinse. Bring a large pot of water to the boil and add the soaked cancha. Boil for 2 hours, or until no longer hard and starchy. Drain the cooked cancha and spread out to dry on paper towels.

■ Heat the oil in a deep, heavy frying pot or Dutch oven to 375°F on a deep-fry thermometer. The oil should come no more than a third of the way up the sides of the pan. Add about 1 cup of the cooked cancha and fry for 10 minutes, or until the kernels stop sputtering and start crackling (in other words, until the water inside has cooked off as steam). Scoop the cancha from the oil using a skimmer or slotted spoon, and drain on paper towels. While still hot, sprinkle with kosher salt. Repeat until all the cancha is cooked. Store in a tightly sealed container for up to 1 month.

Boniato Stars

Boniato *is a firm, extra-starchy tuber with golden flesh.
In flavor and texture, it's somewhere between a sweet
potato and a potato. I have a special method for making
star-shaped boniato chips to garnish ceviche. If you don't
want to go to the trouble of cutting the stars, thinly sliced
boniato still makes extraordinarily good chips, if not
quite as dramatic a presentation.*

SERVES 8 AS A SNACK

2 boniatos (see Special Ingredients)
1 quart pure peanut oil, for frying
Kosher salt
Freshly ground black pepper

■ Trim off about ½ inch from the ends of the boniatos,
and pare into fairly even oblong shapes. As the boniatos
are cut, place them immediately into a bowl of cold water
to keep them from discoloring. Cut crosswise into thin,
even slices, ⅛ inch thick. Stack the slices about 1½ inches
high. Cut triangle-shaped wedges out of the edges of the
boniatos, cutting between 8 and 10 wedges from each
boniato round. You should have star-shaped pieces left.

■ You will need 2 wire cooling racks and 2 large metal
paper clamps. Drain the boniato stars and place a layer
on one side of the rack. Cover with a second rack,
top-side down. Clamp shut with the 2 clamps.

■ In a skillet that is larger in diameter than the racks, heat
the oil to 375°F on a deep-fry thermometer. Carefully
lower the rack into the oil and fry until the boniato stars
are lightly and evenly browned. Remove the racks from
the oil and drain. When they're cool enough to handle,
remove the clamps. Sprinkle the boniato stars with salt
and pepper, and serve as a garnish for ceviche.

Boniato

The boniato or tropical sweet potato, also known as
batata, camote, or Cuban sweet potato, is a member of the
morning glory family. Boniatos are used just as you would
a regular sweet potato; they resemble a cross between a
baking potato and a sweet potato. They have patchy,
pink- to burgundy-colored skin, with white or cream-
colored flesh. When cooked, boniatos are fluffier, drier,
and less sweet than the yellow- or orange-fleshed sweet
potato. Look for boniatos in Latino and Asian markets,
and choose those that are firm and heavy for their size.

They should be rock-hard, with no soft or moldy spots,
because they are prone to bruising and rapid spoilage.
Keep them in a cool, dark place, but not in the refrigerator,
and avoid any that are soft or wrinkled, or that feel light
for their size. Boniatos are available year-round, although
scarce in February and March. When preparing boniatos,
drop them into cold water immediately, as the flesh
discolors quickly. When cooking, keep the boniato
completely covered with water, or gray and blue blotches
may appear.

Basic Béchamel Sauce

This thick cream sauce is used as the base for many different croquetas. You can improvise by combining the sauce, which is the binder, with other firm (not watery) ingredients such as diced cheese, diced roast chicken or pork, cooked sausage bits, caramelized onion, cooked starchy vegetables (such as boniato, taro, sweet potato, and yuca), or roasted pepper bits both hot and sweet.

MAKES 2 CUPS

5 tablespoons unsalted butter (if using salted butter, reduce the amount of salt to 1 teaspoon)

¼ cup diced onion

5 tablespoons unbleached flour

2 cups whole milk, scalded in a small pan on the stove or in a glass measuring cup in the microwave

2 teaspoons kosher salt

½ teaspoon freshly grated nutmeg

½ teaspoon ground white pepper

1 tablespoon butter, cut into bits, for storage

■ In a small, nonreactive (stainless-steel or enameled) saucepan, melt the butter until sizzling. Add the onion and cook 3 to 4 minutes, or until soft but not brown. Whisk in the flour and cook for 5 minutes over low heat to eliminate the raw taste from the flour. While constantly whisking, pour in the scalded milk, and continue whisking until the sauce is smooth. Bring to the boil over moderate heat, whisking often, especially where the edges of the pan bottom meet the sides. Add the salt, nutmeg, and pepper, and cook over low heat for 5 minutes until smooth and thickened. Using an immersion blender, purée the sauce until smooth.

■ Using a heat-resistant spatula, scrape the sauce from the pan and transfer to a container—preferably tall and narrow so less surface area is exposed. Whisk again to ensure that the sauce is smooth. Dot the top with the butter bits, which should melt and cover the top with a thin, protective coating. Cool to room temperature; then cover and refrigerate until ready to use, up to 1 week.

Rice Croquetas

I use these simple croquetas made with cooked rice to garnish my Marinated Grilled Chilean Sea Bass Ceviche. They are also good served with cocktails and accompanied by a spicy dipping sauce such as the Smoked Corn–Amarillo Vinaigrette (see recipe on page 154). I recommend cooking the rice and the Basic Béchamel Sauce 1 or 2 days ahead of time so that both are well chilled. If you neglect to chill the rice and sauce, the croquetas will be mushy.

SERVES 8 AS A GARNISH, OR ABOUT 16 CROQUETAS

¼ cup olive oil

½ cup finely diced onion

1 cup long-grain white rice

1 cup water, simmering

2 teaspoons kosher salt

½ cup Basic Béchamel Sauce, chilled (see recipe on page 140)

1 cup unbleached flour

3 eggs, lightly beaten

1 cup fine dry bread crumbs

2 cups pure peanut oil, for frying

■ In a medium-heavy saucepan, heat the olive oil until sizzling. Add the onion and cook until soft but not brown, about 5 minutes. Stir in the rice and cook 1 or 2 minutes, or until the rice is shiny but not brown. Add the simmering water and salt and bring the mixture to the boil. Reduce the heat to a slow simmer, cover, and cook 15 minutes, or until the liquid has been absorbed by the rice. Remove from heat and spread out on a large, flat pan to cool quickly. Refrigerate the rice until cold, about 30 minutes or as much as 2 days ahead of time.

■ Combine the chilled rice with the chilled Basic Béchamel Sauce. Scoop into small balls, about 1 tablespoon each, and place on a tray lined with waxed paper. Refrigerate about 15 minutes; then wet your hands in cold water and roll the balls to shape them.

■ Place the flour in one bowl, the eggs in a second bowl, and the bread crumbs in a third bowl. Dust the croquetas with the flour, coating evenly and shaking off the excess. Next, roll in the egg, allowing the excess liquid to drain off. Finally roll in the bread crumbs, coating evenly and shaking off the excess. Spread out in a single layer on a waxed paper–lined tray and refrigerate until ready to fry, at least 1 hour and up to 24 hours ahead of time.

■ In a deep, heavy frying pot or Dutch oven, heat the oil to 375°F on a deep-fry thermometer. One by one, carefully place the croquetas in the oil. Don't drop them into the oil, because it is likely to spatter. Work in batches, if necessary—you don't want to crowd them. Each croqueta should be surrounded by oil. Fry about 5 minutes, or until deep golden brown on all sides, turning so they cook evenly. Using a slotted spoon or wire skimmer, scoop the croquetas from the oil, drain on paper towels, and serve immediately.

Goat Cheese Croquetas

These delicious goat cheese croquetas couldn't be easier to make, because you don't need any binder. I love the mild goat cheese made by Laura Chenel in California and by Coach Farms in New York state, but you could also use an imported French Montrachet or Israeli Silver Goat. Aged goat cheese is too strong-tasting to use here.

SERVES 8 AS A GARNISH,
OR ABOUT 16 CROQUETAS

¾ pound mild goat cheese, crumbled
2 cachucha chiles, seeded and finely minced
    (see Special Ingredients)
2 teaspoons kosher salt
½ teaspoon freshly ground black pepper
1 cup unbleached flour
3 eggs, lightly beaten
1 cup fine dry bread crumbs
2 cups pure peanut oil, for frying

■ Place the goat cheese in a small bowl and mash with a fork. Add the chiles, salt, and pepper, and mash again to combine well. Scoop into small balls, about 1 tablespoon each, and place on a tray lined with waxed paper. Refrigerate about 15 minutes; then wet your hands in cold water and roll the balls to shape them. Place the flour in one bowl, the eggs in a second bowl, and the bread crumbs in a third bowl. Roll the balls in the flour, coating evenly and shaking off the excess. Next roll in the egg, allowing the excess liquid to drain off. Finally, roll in the bread crumbs, coating evenly and shaking off the excess. Spread out in a single layer on a waxed paper–lined tray and refrigerate until ready to fry, at least one hour and up to 24 hours ahead of time.

■ In a deep, heavy frying pot or Dutch oven, heat the oil to 375°F on a deep-fry thermometer. One by one, lay the croquetas in the oil. Don't drop them into the oil because it is likely to spatter. Work in batches, if necessary—you don't want to crowd the croquetas. Each croqueta should be surrounded by oil. Fry about 5 minutes, or until deep golden brown on all sides, turning so they cook evenly. Using a slotted spoon or wire skimmer, scoop the croquetas from the oil, drain on paper towels, and serve immediately.

Goat Cheese–Stuffed Cachucha Chiles

Here I stuff mild cachucha chiles with mild goat cheese, coat them in bread crumbs, then fry them until crunchy. I serve them as a garnish for my Jumbo Lump Crab Ceviche with Tomatillo Salsa (see recipe on page 102), but they would be equally good as a bocadito, *a "little mouthful" to serve with drinks.*

SERVES 8 AS A GARNISH

¼ pound mild goat cheese, crumbled

1 teaspoon kosher salt

½ teaspoon freshly ground black pepper

8 cachucha chiles (see Special Ingredients)

1 cup unbleached flour

3 eggs, lightly beaten

1 cup fine dry bread crumbs

2 cups pure peanut oil, for frying

■ Place the goat cheese in a small bowl and mash with a fork. Add the salt and pepper, and mash again to combine well. Scoop into 8 small balls and refrigerate about 15 minutes.

■ Meanwhile, cut a slit lengthwise along one side of each chile. Carefully dig out and discard the seeds and spongy white membrane. Gently pull apart the chiles to open them up without breaking them. Fill each chile with a portion of the goat cheese and then press the edges together. (If you've gotten goat cheese on the outside of the chiles, wipe it off so that you have a clean surface.)

■ Place the flour in one bowl, the eggs in a second bowl, and the bread crumbs in a third bowl. Dust the stuffed chiles with the flour, coating evenly and shaking off the excess. Next, roll in the egg, allowing the excess liquid to drain off. Finally, roll in the bread crumbs, coating evenly and shaking off the excess. Spread out in a single layer on a waxed paper–lined tray and refrigerate until ready to fry, at least 1 hour and up to 24 hours ahead of time.

■ In a deep, heavy frying pot or Dutch oven, heat the oil to 375°F on a deep-fry thermometer. One by one, lay the stuffed chiles in the oil. Don't drop them into the oil, because it is likely to spatter. Work in batches, if necessary—you don't want to crowd the pan. Each chile should be surrounded by oil. Fry about 5 minutes, or until deep golden brown on all sides, turning so they cook evenly. Using a slotted spoon or wire skimmer, scoop the chiles from the oil, drain on paper towels, and serve immediately.

Spinach–Pine Nut Croquetas

Pine nuts are associated with the Native American cultures of New Mexico and Arizona. Although they are not common in South America, I think their sweet, rich nuttiness is too good to ignore. Here I use them to make a crunchy crust for creamy, spinach-filled croquetas.

SERVES 8 AS A GARNISH,
OR ABOUT 16 CROQUETAS

½ cup Basic Béchamel Sauce, chilled (see recipe
   on page 140)
1 cup chopped, cooked spinach, all liquid squeezed out
½ cup pine nuts
½ cup fine dry bread crumbs
½ cup unbleached flour
3 eggs, lightly beaten
2 cups vegetable oil, for frying

■ In a large bowl, combine the Basic Béchamel Sauce with the spinach. Scoop into small balls, about 1 tablespoon each, and place on a tray lined with waxed paper. Refrigerate about 15 minutes; then wet your hands in cold water and roll the balls to shape them. Place the pine nuts and bread crumbs in the bowl of a food processor, and process to obtain a fine, dry mixture. Place the flour in one bowl, the eggs in a second bowl, and the bread crumb mixture in a third bowl. Roll the balls in the flour, coating evenly and shaking off the excess. Next roll in the egg, allowing the excess liquid to drain off. Finally, roll in the pine nut–bread crumb mixture, coating evenly and shaking off the excess. Spread out on a single layer on a waxed paper–lined tray and refrigerate until ready to fry, at least one hour and up to 24 hours ahead of time.

■ In a deep, heavy frying pot or Dutch oven, heat the oil to 375°F on a frying thermometer. One by one, lay the croquetas in the oil. Don't drop them into the oil, because it is likely to spatter. Work in batches, if necessary—you don't want to crowd them. Each croqueta should be surrounded by oil. Fry about 5 minutes, or until deep golden brown on all sides, turning so they cook evenly. Using a slotted spoon or wire skimmer, scoop the croquetas from the oil, drain on paper towels, and serve immediately.

Fried Yuca Spears

Beloved throughout the Caribbean, Central America, and South America, yuca (also known as cassava and manioc) is basically a bland, starchy root. What makes it good is its creamy, rich texture—as long as it is prepared properly. There is a set of unpleasantly tough strings running down the center of the root. To remove these, I pare the yuca, cut it into manageable lengths, and quarter the pieces lengthwise. I then cut away and discard the inner quarter of the yuca, which contains the strings.

SERVES 6

3 quarts water
1 cup white vinegar
2 tablespoons kosher salt, plus more for seasoning
2 large yucas, pared and inner core trimmed
1 quart pure peanut oil, for frying

■ In a large pot, bring the water, vinegar, and 2 tablespoons salt to the boil. Add the yuca spears and boil for 15 to 20 minutes, or until tender when pierced with a fork.

■ Have ready a large bowl of ice mixed with water. Drain the yuca and plunge immediately into the ice water. This will encourage the yuca spears to spread open on their inner sides, creating a creamier texture. Drain, cover, and refrigerate for up to 2 days, until ready to fry.

■ In a large, deep frying pot or Dutch oven, heat the oil to 375°F on a deep-fry thermometer. Working in batches, add only enough yuca spears so that there is plenty of bubbling oil surrounding them. Fry until golden brown and crisp, about 8 minutes, turning so they cook evenly. Scoop from the oil, drain on paper towels, sprinkle with kosher salt, and serve immediately.

Yuca

Those long, brown-skinned roots (usually sold waxed for preservation) are called yuca, cassava, manioc, or mandioca, depending on where you come from in Latin America. Originally from Brazil, where it is known as *aipim*, yuca was first domesticated by Amazonian peoples thousands of years ago. You may not realize you've eaten yuca, but it is the source of all tapioca. There are two basic kinds of yuca: sweet and bitter. The sweet variety, the one sold in American supermarkets, is very starchy and once it has been boiled or fried can be eaten as is. The bitter yuca must first be pounded, rinsed, and strained several times to remove the bitter poison cyanide before it can be converted into edible flour.

Fresh Coconut Shavings

The key to choosing a good coconut is to examine it carefully. You shouldn't see any moldy spots or detect any fermented aroma. Shake the coconut. You should hear plenty of liquid sloshing around. Once the coconut ripens, the liquid it contains loses the sweet creaminess it has when the fruit is green. Most people discard this liquid.

MAKES ABOUT 2 CUPS

1 large, fresh coconut, full of liquid

■ The coconut has three "eyes," one of which is soft. This is the one you want to poke open, using an awl or a sharpening steel. Drain the coconut liquid, and discard it. Don't skip this step, because you will be baking the coconut next. If it's not drained, the coconut could explode.

■ Preheat the oven to 350°F. Bake the coconut for 25 minutes; then cool. The flesh will shrink away from the shell. Break it open by hitting with a heavy hammer across its "equator." The shell pieces will pop away, leaving a thin layer of dark skin on the flesh. I like to keep this dark skin on the coconut for its natural look, although some people prefer to pare it away.

■ I prefer to cut ring-shaped shavings of coconut for garnish. First, cut the coconut in half through the "equator." Then slice it very thinly, using a mandoline, Benriner cutter, or deli slicer. You can also shred the coconut using the medium or coarse shredding side of a sharp box grater. Use the coconut to garnish and add a little fresh crunch to ceviche. Store the coconut shavings in the refrigerator in an airtight container for up to 1 week. The coconut shavings should be covered with water. Drain before using.

Crunchy Vanilla Beans

Vanilla is the only orchid that produces edible fruit, in the form of seed pods. The plants grow near the equator in exotic locales such as Madagascar, Mexico, Tahiti, Indonesia, and Bali. It takes five to six pounds of freshly picked pods to make one pound of vanilla beans, which are cured either in the air or over a fire. The result is black, oily, smooth pods with a delectable fragrance.

SERVES 4 AS A GARNISH

2 plump, supple vanilla beans, halved lengthwise
1 cup water
¼ cup sugar
¼ teaspoon cayenne

■ Scrape the tiny vanilla seeds and their dark, gooey pulp from the beans. Reserve the seeds and pulp for another recipe, or mix with ½ cup brandy or whiskey and use as vanilla extract.

■ Preheat the oven to 300°F. Bring a small saucepan of water to the boil. Add the vanilla beans and boil for about 15 minutes, or until soft and tender. Empty the pan; then fill it with 1 cup water, and add the sugar and the vanilla beans. Bring to a boil, reduce the heat to moderate, and boil for about 10 minutes, or until shiny and glazed.

■ Drain off any remaining syrup (saving it for another use if desired, such as poaching fruit or sweetening iced tea) and spread out the beans in a small baking pan. Bake for 15 minutes, or until crisp, dark, and shiny. Remove from the oven and sprinkle with cayenne. Store at room temperature in an airtight container for up to 1 week. Serve as a garnish.

Crispy Japanese Eggplant Chips

Choose the long, thin Asian eggplants here, for they are mild and creamy with tiny, inconspicuous seeds. The Chinese variety has a purple calyx, while the Japanese is topped with green. They are almost always available at Asian markets and should be firm and smooth, with no soft spots. For this recipe, you will need parchment paper or, even better, two sheets of Silpat, the "magic" French silicone-based mats for baking. Silpat sheets, available from many kitchen stores and gourmet catalogs, can be used hundreds of times. You will also need an inexpensive plastic spray bottle for the syrup.

MAKES ABOUT 16 EGGPLANT CHIPS, ENOUGH TO SERVE 8 AS A GARNISH

1½ cups water
1½ cups sugar
1 pound Japanese or Chinese eggplant, stem ends removed
2 teaspoons kosher salt
½ teaspoon cayenne

■ In a medium saucepan, combine the water and sugar, and bring to the boil. Boil 1 or 2 minutes, until the syrup is clear; then remove from the heat. When cool, transfer about half the liquid to a clean plastic spray bottle, pouring the remainder into a bowl.

■ Slice the eggplants lengthwise as thinly and evenly as possible, preferably using a Benriner cutter or mandoline. Preheat the oven to 200°F.

■ Dip each eggplant slice into the sugar syrup and place in a single layer on baking sheets lined with parchment or Silpat sheets. Bake 1 hour, turning once, spraying every 10 minutes with the sugar syrup to make a shiny glaze, or until lightly browned and shiny.

■ While still warm and flexible, remove the eggplant chips from the pans so that the cooling sugar doesn't stick. Combine the salt and cayenne, and lightly dust the eggplant chips with the mixture. Store in an airtight container in a cool, dry place for up to 2 days before serving.

Popped Pepitas

I pan-roast pepitas, or green pumpkin seeds, in a dry skillet to bring out their rich nutty flavor. These pepitas make a positively addictive bocadito (or "little mouthful") to enjoy with cocktails. Natural-foods stores are the best places to buy raw pepitas. Though you can find already toasted pepitas, the flavor and crunch will be much better if you make your own.

SERVES 8 AS A GARNISH

½ pound raw green pepitas
Juice of ½ lemon
1 teaspoon kosher salt

■ Preheat a large cast-iron or steel skillet for about 5 minutes, or until the skillet begins to get white. Add the pepitas, and toast, tossing continuously until they puff up and pop (a little like popcorn). They will lose their flatness and become round and browned. Continue to cook about 8 minutes or until the pepitas are all lightly browned and popped. Remove the skillet from the heat, add the lemon juice, and toss vigorously to coat the pepitas with the juice. Toss with the salt, remove from the pan, and either serve immediately or store in an airtight container for up to 3 days.

SALSAS AND
VINAIGRETTES

Grilled Corn Salsa

This grilled corn salsa is so fabulous you'll find yourself serving it again and again. I especially like it as a topping for my cold-smoked salmon ceviche, but it's also a winner spooned over grilled oily fish such as bluefish, tuna, Chilean sea bass, or Boston mackerel. "Chipotles in adobo" are ripe red jalapeños that have been dried over a wood fire, giving them a smoky flavor. They are then packed in a tomato-based sauce with other seasonings. Buy chipotles in adobo in small cans at some supermarkets or at Mexican groceries. I prefer La Morena brand, which contains the purest ingredients.

MAKES 4 CUPS

7 ears of corn, husked
1¾ cups fresh lime juice
1 bunch fresh cilantro leaves
4 serrano chiles, seeded and minced
1 teaspoon chopped chipotles in adobo
5 tablespoons olive oil
1 tablespoon sherry vinegar
2 red onions, cut into small dice and rinsed in cold water
2 red bell peppers, seeded and cut into small dice
5 plum tomatoes, seeded and cut into small dice

■ Preheat a grill to red-hot. Add the corn and grill evenly until well browned and slightly charred. When cool enough to handle, cut off the kernels without cutting too close to the cob. In a medium bowl, combine the corn with the lime juice, cilantro, serranos, chipotles, olive oil, vinegar, onions, bell peppers, and tomatoes. Serve at once, or cover and refrigerate for up to 3 days.

Pico de Gallo Salsa

Pico de gallo translates as "rooster's beak" because of the brilliant red color of the sauce. This spicy salsa keeps up to two days in the refrigerator. Be sure to drain off any excess liquid before serving. Roma or plum tomatoes are firmer and have fewer seeds than round or beefsteak tomatoes and are therefore the best in this salsa.

MAKES ABOUT 4 CUPS

1 small red onion, peeled and cut into very fine dice (about ¾ cup)
1½ pounds plum tomatoes with seeds, cut into very fine dice (about 3 cups tomatoes)
2 serrano chiles, trimmed and processed to a chunky paste with seeds (about 2 tablespoons)
2 tablespoons fresh lime juice
½ cup chiffonade of cilantro
2 teaspoons kosher salt

■ Place the diced onion in a bowl of cold water and swish around to remove surface acids. Drain well. In a medium nonreactive (stainless-steel or enameled) bowl, combine the onion, tomatoes, chiles, lime juice, cilantro, and salt. Serve at once, or cover and refrigerate.

Huitlacoche Vinaigrette

I'm crazy about huitlacoche, *although you might think I'm just crazy when you know that it is actually a fungus that grows inside corn kernels. Huitlacoche is purple-black in color, with an earthy, slightly sweet flavor reminiscent of truffles (sometimes it is called "corn truffle," although that is a bit of a stretch) and black trumpet mushrooms. I buy it from a farmer in Florida who raises nothing but this Mexican delicacy—see Special Ingredients for more information.*

MAKES ABOUT 2 CUPS

1 shallot, peeled and chopped
3 cloves garlic, chopped
2 tablespoons vegetable oil
6 tablespoons huitlacoche, defrosted if frozen
    (see Special Ingredients)
⅓ cup balsamic vinegar
2 tablespoons sherry vinegar
¼ cup extra virgin olive oil
1 teaspoon chopped fresh thyme
¼ teaspoon freshly ground black pepper
1 tablespoon kosher salt
½ cup fresh lime juice

■ In a small skillet, sauté the shallot and garlic in the vegetable oil until soft but not brown. Add the huitlacoche and cook 5 minutes, or until most of the liquid has cooked away. Remove from the heat, and cool. Scrape the mixture into a blender jar. Blend to a smooth purée; then slowly pour in the vinegars, oil, thyme, pepper, salt, and lime juice, blending until smooth and creamy. Serve at once, or cover and refrigerate for up to 1 week.

Japanese Mirin Dressing

Mirin is a sweet, concentrated Japanese rice wine used for cooking. Hontari, the brand I use, contains no alcohol, which I like because alcohol would react with the fish and "cook" it. This dressing must steep for one week so that the flavors have a chance to be absorbed by the mirin.

MAKES 1 CUP

1 cup mirin, preferably Hontari brand
½ cup thinly sliced ginger
2 scallions, thinly sliced
1 tablespoon chopped red onion
1 tablespoon chopped cilantro

■ In a clean jar, combine the mirin, ginger, scallions, onion, and cilantro. Cover and refrigerate for 1 week. Strain through a sieve, discarding the solids, and refrigerate until ready to use, up to 1 week.

Smoked Corn–Amarillo Vinaigrette

Amarillo is Spanish for "yellow." Here it refers to a yellow chile that is used extensively in Peru. I explain how to make your own simple stovetop hot smoker, but feel free to use an electric smoker if you have one. In Peru, they use eucalyptus wood for smoking. It's very difficult to obtain in this country, so I use hickory or cherry wood. Many kinds of wood chips are good for smoking as long as they have no additives, but mesquite has too dominant a flavor to use here. When hot-smoking, keep the smoke light and airy. If it is heavy and white in color, it means that the temperature is too hot, and will impart a bitter taste to whatever you're smoking.

MAKES 3 CUPS

2 ears corn, with husk

2 tablespoons butter

2 cups yellow corn kernels cut from 3 ears corn
   (or 2 cups frozen yellow corn kernels, rinsed)

½ teaspoon turmeric

¼ cup champagne vinegar

2 teaspoons Peruvian amarillo chile purée
   (see Special Ingredients)

1 tablespoon kosher salt

½ cup mild olive oil

■ Have ready a rectangular or circular metal pan, such as a cake pan or roasting pan, at least 3 inches deep. You will also need a wire cooling rack approximately the same size as the pan, or you can improvise with a perforated screen. Spread a thin layer of wood chips in the bottom of the pan. Form aluminum foil into 4 lumps about the size of tennis balls. Place one foil ball at each corner of the pan, on top of the wood chips. Lay the wire rack on top. Place the 2 ears of corn in their husks on top of the rack. Set the pan over moderate heat until smoke starts to rise from the chips. Cover the pan tightly with aluminum foil and reduce the heat to low. Hot-smoke for about 10 minutes, or until the corn has a definite smoked aroma. Remove the smoker from the heat. Husk the corn. Cut off the kernels and reserve.

■ In a medium skillet, melt the butter over moderate heat. Add the smoked and fresh corn kernels. To release the sugars in the corn, cook for about 10 minutes, or until thoroughly cooked but not browned. Add the turmeric during the last few minutes of cooking. Remove the pan from the heat and cool.

■ Scrape the corn into the container of a blender and add the vinegar, amarillo chile purée, and salt. Blend until smooth, add the olive oil, and blend again. Strain the vinaigrette through a sieve to remove the corn skins. Use at once, or cover and refrigerate for up to 3 days.

Blood Orange Sauce

Although blood oranges grew in America early in the last century, people were supposedly so frightened of them that cultivation ceased. About twenty years ago, when American chefs started on their world travels, they became enamored of the tangy, brilliantly colored oranges. At first we only saw blood oranges imported from Italy, especially Sicily. In the last five to ten years, California citrus growers have been producing them once again. You could also squeeze fresh blood oranges and reduce the juice to about half the original amount. Straight juice won't have the concentrated flavor I'm looking for here. Goya Foods, the largest Hispanic-owned food company in the United States, and La Fe Company both produce 14-ounce packages of frozen passion fruit purée, sold in many Latin supermarkets.

MAKES ABOUT 3 CUPS

6 tablespoons blood orange concentrate
   (see Special Ingredients)
6 tablespoons fresh orange juice
2 tablespoons fresh lime juice
6 tablespoons passion fruit purée
   (see Special Ingredients)
1 tablespoon ketchup
¼ habanero chile, seeded
2 teaspoons kosher salt
½ red onion, peeled and cut into tiny dice
2 tablespoons sliced fresh mint

■ In a medium nonreactive (stainless-steel or enameled) bowl, combine the blood orange concentrate, orange juice, lime juice, passion fruit purée, ketchup, chile, salt, onion, and mint. Use at once, or cover and refrigerate for up to 4 days. If you plan to store the dressing more than 1 day, add the mint just before serving, to retain its bright color and fresh aroma.

Lime Allioli

Allioli from Spain's Mediterranean coast and aioli *from Provence in southern France share a common ancestry. The French sauce is a rich, garlic-laden mayonnaise, while the Spanish version has little or no garlic and lots of citrus for zing. The best zester to use is called a microplane. It will remove only a thin layer of zest with none of the bitter pith.*

MAKES ABOUT 1½ CUPS

2 egg yolks (*see note, below)
½ teaspoon honey
1 teaspoon salt
1 cup vegetable oil
¼ cup fresh lime juice
½ teaspoon lime zest (green part only)
1 teaspoon Natural Green Coloring
   (optional; see recipe on page 187)

■ In a small bowl, whisk together the yolks, honey, and salt. Drizzle in the vegetable oil while whisking constantly. Continue to beat in about half the oil until it has been absorbed. Now beat in about half the lime juice, zest, and the optional Natural Green Coloring. Beat in the remaining oil and thin the sauce by beating in the remaining lime juice. Taste for seasoning, cover, and refrigerate until ready to serve.

Note: Because this recipe yields a relatively small amount of sauce, it is better to make it by hand. If you double the recipe, you can prepare it using a food processor: Place the yolks, honey, and salt in the bowl of the processor. Process lightly until the mixture is sticky, then start beating in the oil. Continue as in the directions above. Thin with a little lukewarm water to desired consistency.

*Because of the slight risk of salmonella, raw eggs should not be served to the very young, the ill or elderly, or pregnant women.

Sour Orange Mojo

Called mojo *in Spanish and* molho *in Brazilian Portuguese, this tangy sauce is made in any number of ways. Once made, it will keep indefinitely if refrigerated. It is traditional to serve boiled or fried yuca with mojo poured over the top while the yuca is still hot. I've adapted the traditional recipe, which is chunky with a julienne of red onion. Instead, I purée the sauce for a smooth texture. Seville orange or sour orange is the best juice to use here, but it can be hard to come by and also expensive. I substitute orange juice mixed with lime juice for a similar flavor. You can often buy sour orange juice in Hispanic markets, and sometimes you can find fresh sour oranges in season.*

MAKES 1 QUART, ENOUGH FOR 16 SERVINGS

2 quarts fresh orange juice
2 cups fresh lime juice
1 white onion, roughly chopped
2 tablespoons kosher salt
1 cup extra virgin olive oil
2 tablespoons chopped garlic

■ In a large nonreactive (stainless-steel or enameled) saucepan, bring the orange juice, lime juice, onion, and salt to the boil. Reduce the heat to moderate and cook until the liquid has reduced by half.

■ In a small skillet, heat ¼ cup of olive oil. Add the garlic and cook until lightly browned. Pour the garlic and oil into the reduced orange juice mixture, along with the remaining ¾ cup olive oil. Blend the mixture until smooth; then cool. Cover and refrigerate until ready to use.

Tobiko Wasabi Vinaigrette

Japanese tobiko wasabi, *crisp little beads of flying-fish roe that glitter and add texture when used as a garnish, has become the latest rage. The tobiko roe, which usually has a reddish tint and a slight hint of brininess, is now available in a range of colors and flavors, including pale green, spiked with wasabi.*

MAKES ½ CUP

2 tablespoons fresh lime juice
1 tablespoon sherry vinegar
5 tablespoons mild olive oil
½ teaspoon kosher salt
½ teaspoon prepared wasabi paste
2 teaspoons tobiko caviar
½ teaspoon chiffonade of culantro (or cilantro)

■ Whisk together the lime juice, vinegar, olive oil, salt, and wasabi until smooth. Stir in the tobiko caviar and culantro. Cover and refrigerate until ready to use.

Wasabi

Wasabi is most often encountered as a mound of green paste accompanying sushi. Real wasabi, *Wasabia japonica*, is one of the rarest and most difficult vegetables in the world to grow. The plant is highly valued in Japanese cuisine, where it is used primarily as a condiment for seafood dishes. While hot to the taste, unlike chile peppers wasabi is not long-lived on the palate and its heat quickly subsides into an extremely pleasant, mild vegetable flavor. Because less expensive ingredients are sometimes used to fill out a package of wasabi, check the label to be sure that it is the main ingredient.

Three Chile Orange Sauce

You'll need three different kinds of whole dried chiles to make this versatile sauce. The recipe makes a rather large quantity, but because it keeps very well, it's a welcome addition to your pantry. Use it to dress hot smoked squid, as in the recipe for Hot Smoked Squid Ceviche with Chayote Escabeche, Three Chile Orange Sauce on page 100, or serve it with grilled chicken, duck breast, or turkey breast cutlets. Turn to Special Ingredients and Tools for sources for the chiles.

MAKES 2 QUARTS

3 whole dried ancho chiles (see Special Ingredients)
3 whole dried guajillo chiles
3 whole dried New Mexico red chiles
3 quarts fresh orange juice
3 tablespoons kosher salt

■ Cut open the chiles. Remove and discard the seed pods, surrounding membranes, and stems. Place in a large, dry skillet over moderately high heat and toast, shaking the skillet, until the chiles start to give off a strong aroma and are lightly browned. Be careful not to burn them.

■ Pour the orange juice into a large nonreactive (stainless-steel or enameled) saucepan and add the toasted chiles and salt. Bring to the boil; then reduce heat to a simmer. Cook slowly for 30 minutes, or until the chiles are completely soft, and let cool until cool enough to handle. Using an immersion blender, purée the mixture in the pan and strain it through a sieve into a bowl. Wipe the pan to clean any remaining seeds, and return the chile-orange purée to the pan. Bring back to the boil; then reduce the heat to low, and simmer 30 minutes longer, or until slightly thickened. Transfer to a clean container, cool, cover, and refrigerate. Rewarm over low heat, stirring so the sauce doesn't stick.

ESCABECHES
AND SALADS

Haitian Eggplant Salad

There may be a long list of ingredients for this well-flavored salad, but most are readily available and inexpensive. It can be prepared one or two days ahead of time, but add the scallions, parsley, and cilantro just before serving, for freshness. Be sure to taste for seasoning, especially if you make the salad ahead, because flavors do start to fade in a day or two. This salad is outstanding spread on crostini or crackers as a quick hors d'oeuvre.

MAKES ABOUT 3 CUPS SALAD

2 large, firm eggplants
2 tablespoons kosher salt
1 cup small diced red bell peppers
2 tablespoons finely diced ginger root
1 tablespoon chopped Japanese pickled ginger
2 tablespoons minced habanero chile
2 tablespoons natural sesame seeds, lightly toasted
½ cup balsamic vinegar
6 tablespoons extra virgin olive oil
1 tablespoon Japanese toasted sesame oil
2 tablespoons fresh lime juice
¼ cup thinly sliced scallions
2 tablespoons chopped Italian parsley
2 tablespoons chopped cilantro

■ Bring a pot with 2 quarts of water and 1 tablespoon of the salt to the boil. Trim and completely peel the eggplants. Cut into slices about 1 inch thick. Add to the pot and bring the water back to the boil. Reduce the heat to moderate and cook for about 30 minutes, or until the eggplant is thoroughly tender when pierced with a fork. Drain well, cool, and finely chop the eggplant by hand.

■ In a medium bowl, combine the red bell peppers, ginger root, pickled ginger, habanero, sesame seeds, vinegar, olive oil, sesame oil, lime juice, and remaining salt with the chopped eggplant. If serving immediately, add the scallions, parsley, and cilantro. Otherwise, cover and refrigerate for the next day, and add the scallions, parsley, and cilantro just before serving.

Red Pearl Onion Escabeche

Make these pickled and spiced pearl onions up to three weeks before you want to use them. They are also delicious served with cold meats such as sliced roast turkey, pork, or beef. The only difficult part is the rather tedious task of peeling the onions.

MAKES 1 QUART

2 pint containers red pearl onions

1 cup sherry vinegar

1 cup water

¼ cup olive oil

¼ cup fresh raspberries (or frozen unsweetened whole raspberries)

3 bay leaves

2 whole cloves

¼ teaspoon allspice

1 habanero chile, cut into quarters and seeded

1 tablespoon sugar

2 teaspoons kosher salt

■ To peel the pearl onions, bring a medium pan of salted water to the boil. Drop in the onions, cook for 2 minutes, and then drain and rinse under cold water. Using scissors, cut off most of the stringy part of the pointed end, leaving enough so that the onion still ends in a point. Using a small sharp knife, cut off the root end flush with the bottom so that the onion layers still remain attached. Slip off and discard the outermost layer of skin on each onion.

■ Meanwhile, combine the remaining ingredients in a medium nonreactive (stainless-steel or enameled) pan and bring to the boil. Reduce the heat and simmer for 20 minutes. Strain through a sieve into a bowl, pressing lightly to extract all the liquid. Discard the solids, wipe the pan clean, and return the strained liquid to the pan. Add the trimmed pearl onions, bring to the boil, and remove from the heat immediately. Cool to room temperature; transfer to a sterilized jar (see To Sterilize Jars for Escabeche on page 124); then cover, and refrigerate for up to 3 weeks.

Green Mango Escabeche

Here I use hard green mangos, which more closely resemble a vegetable than a fruit at this stage, and I slice them paper-thin. Admittedly, it's easier to make this delicious fast pickle in a restaurant, where we have access to a deli slicer. At home, I would recommend using either a mandoline or a Benriner cutter (sold inexpensively in many Asian markets). Unless you're a trained Japanese sushi chef, it's close to impossible to slice the mango thinly enough by hand.

MAKES 1½ CUPS

2 green hard mangos
1 small habanero chile, seeded and finely minced
6 tablespoons mild olive oil
¼ cup fresh lime juice
4 teaspoons finely chopped garlic
2 teaspoons sugar
2 teaspoons kosher salt
¼ cup chopped cilantro

■ Pare away the mango skins. Find the large, flat, tongue-shaped pit in the center of each fruit. Slice each side of the mango into paper-thin shavings paralleling the pit, until your slices get too close to it. Discard the pit section.

■ Whisk together the remaining ingredients and toss with the mango. Cover and refrigerate for at least 30 minutes, up to 2 days. Just before serving, drain the excess liquid from the mango and toss with the cilantro.

Carrot Escabeche

These sweet, hot carrot sticks are a wonderful addition to a simple bocadito ("little mouthful") plate with green and black olives and marinated roasted peppers. They are colorful, tasty, and inexpensive. I use them as an ingredient in my Mussel and Clam Ceviche (see recipe on page 122). Rice wine vinegar is mild and slightly sweet, and because it's clear, it doesn't discolor the carrots.

MAKES 2 QUARTS

1 cup sugar
¼ cup kosher salt
1 tablespoon hot red pepper flakes
2 cups rice wine vinegar
2 cups water
3 pounds carrots, peeled
2 tablespoons chopped garlic

■ Combine the sugar, salt, hot pepper flakes, vinegar, and water in a nonreactive (stainless-steel or enameled) pan and bring to the boil. Cut the carrots into 3-inch lengths, then into quarters to form sticks. Pour the hot liquid over the carrot sticks and garlic. Transfer to a sterilized 2-quart jar (see To Sterilize Jars for Escabeche on page 124). Cover and refrigerate at least 2 weeks to marinate. Once ready, the carrots will keep for 2 months.

Lamb Tongue Escabeche

My inspiration here was the tender, spice-infused pig's feet in escabeche my mother used to make. The key is to cook the lamb tongues at the barest simmer so that they come out tender and firm-textured. If you cook them quickly, they will become stringy. Once cooked, the lamb tongues will keep for about two months when refrigerated in their cooking liquid. Use a stainless-steel spoon to scoop out the tongues as needed so as not to contaminate the liquid with bacteria from your hands.

MAKES ABOUT 1½ POUNDS LAMB TONGUE

1 onion, peeled and cut into thin strips
2 habanero chiles, cut in half lengthwise
4 serrano chiles, cut in half lengthwise
2 tablespoons pickling spice
2 teaspoons white peppercorns
6 bay leaves
3 cups red wine vinegar
4 tablespoons kosher salt
6 cups water
4 whole lamb tongues (about 2 pounds)

■ In a large, nonreactive (stainless-steel or enameled) pot, combine the onion, chiles, pickling spice, peppercorns, bay leaves, vinegar, salt, and water, and bring to the boil. Reduce heat to moderate and cook for 20 minutes. Add the lamb tongues and bring to the boil. Skim off and discard any foam. Reduce heat to a low simmer and cook slowly for 2 hours.

■ Remove the pot from heat and cool. Transfer to a sterilized jar (see instructions on page 124), cover, and refrigerate the lamb tongues in their poaching liquid for at least 1 week before using. To prepare the tongue, use a carrot peeler to remove the outer skin. Cut off and discard the tough, enlarged back portion before using in a recipe.

Pickled Pink Onions

You'll find yourself using these lovely rosy pink onions on all sorts of things, from ceviche to sandwiches. Choose Italian red onions for the best color here—those large, dark purplish-red onions that are flattened in shape.

MAKES 1 CUP

2 large red onions, peeled
1 tablespoon grenadine syrup
¼ cup fresh lime juice
¼ cup distilled white vinegar

■ Cut the onions into thin rings. Combine with the grenadine, lime juice, and vinegar, tossing together vigorously to combine well and to break up the onion slices into individual rings. Transfer to a sterilized jar (see To Sterilize Jars for Escabeche on page 124), cover tightly, and refrigerate for at least 1 hour, or up to 2 days, before using. Drain before serving. The onions will keep at least 1 month.

Garlic Escabeche

To give the garlic enough time to pickle properly, you'll need to start this recipe one week in advance. If you're a true garlic lover, you'll enjoy snacking on these pickled cloves straight from the jar. If you don't want to take the time to peel fresh garlic, use the pre-peeled whole garlic cloves sold in many supermarket produce sections. I also use them as an ingredient in recipes such as Mussel and Clam Ceviche (see recipe on page 122). The garlic will keep quite well for at least 1 month if refrigerated.

MAKES 2 CUPS

½ cup diced small onion
½ cup extra virgin olive oil
1 pound peeled garlic cloves
8 bay leaves
1 tablespoon Mexican oregano
1 cup red wine vinegar
2 tablespoons sugar
1 tablespoon kosher salt
Extra virgin olive oil to cover garlic

■ In a large skillet, sauté the onion in ¼ cup of the olive oil. When the onion is soft but not brown, add the garlic and sauté about 5 minutes, or until the garlic is slightly browned. Add the bay leaves, Mexican oregano, vinegar, sugar, salt, and olive oil, and bring to a boil. Remove from the heat, transfer to a bowl (preferably stainless-steel), and cool the mixture to room temperature.

■ Sterilize a 16-ounce canning jar (see To Sterilize Jars for Escabeche on page 124); then fill the jar close to the top with the garlic mixture. Screw on the lid and leave the garlic to marinate for 1 week refrigerated before using. The garlic will keep well for 1 month as long as you remove the cloves with a stainless-steel spoon. Once you've removed garlic from the jars, add more oil to cover the remaining cloves.

Mexican Oregano

Mexican oregano, *Lippia graveolens* (sometimes known as Mexican sage), is a different plant variety from the more familiar Mediterranean oregano. It is stronger and less sweet, well suited to the spicy, hot, cumin-flavored dishes of Mexico and Central America. It is available in dried form from Mexican groceries and specialty spice companies.

Chayote Escabeche

Here I use chayote or "vegetable pear" in a spicy, crunchy escabeche that is easy to make, versatile, and inexpensive. You can buy the pear-shaped, light green chayote squash in many supermarket produce sections and in any Latino market. The mild and aromatic canela, or soft stick cinnamon, is essential here. The more common hard cinnamon sticks sold in American markets are actually the more pungent cassia, which would be too strong for this mild vegetable escabeche. For more information about canela, see page 82.

MAKES 2 QUARTS

6 chayote, about 4 pounds
1 stick canela (soft stick cinnamon)
1 teaspoon dried thyme
1 teaspoon Mexican oregano
4 bay leaves
2 tablespoons olive oil
1 small onion, diced
10 cloves garlic, peeled
3 serrano chiles, halved
½ cup cider vinegar
2 teaspoons kosher salt
Pinch cumin
Pinch ground cardamom

■ Cut the chayote in half. Using a large spoon, dig out the center seed portions and surrounding soft membrane, and discard. Cut each half into 4 wedges and reserve.

■ In a dry pan, toast the cinnamon, thyme, Mexican oregano, and bay leaves over medium heat until the spices give off their aroma and begin to brown. In a large skillet, heat the olive oil over high heat. Add the onion, garlic, chiles, and chayote. Sear over high heat, tossing to cook evenly. Pour the vinegar into the pan and deglaze, shaking to combine the ingredients.

■ Add the salt, cumin, and cardamom, as well as the toasted cinnamon-herb mixture, and shake again. Remove the pan from the heat and transfer the escabeche to a clean container. Cool; transfer to a sterilized jar (see To Sterilize Jars for Escabeche on page 124), then cover and refrigerate. Store for at least 2 days before using. The chayote escabeche will keep for 1 month when refrigerated.

Chayote

Chayote squash, a member of the *Cucurbita* family, goes by many regional names, including vegetable pear, mirliton, and christophene. Many supermarkets now carry chayote, which is quite firm, shaped like a plump pear, and light green in color. It is delicious stuffed and baked or, as in this dish, raw and cut into julienne strips for a juicy crunch. Chayote needn't be peeled before cutting or shredding. When you bake chayote, the skin usually becomes tender enough to eat. If the skin is too stringy when baked or boiled, scoop out the tender flesh and discard the skin.

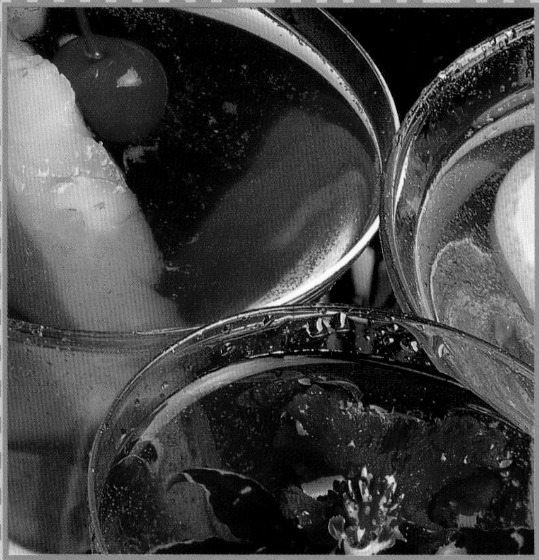

COCKTAILS

Mango Daiquiri

The daiquiri, long a favorite in Cuba, became popular with Americans when an engineer named Jennings Cox was sent to Daiquiri, on the east coast of Cuba, to work in the iron mines. He and his colleagues developed a fondness for the drink there. Cox's friend, Admiral Lucius Johnson, introduced the cocktail to the Army and Navy Club in Washington, D.C., which now has a Daiquiri Lounge. The daiquiri was JFK's preferred cocktail. At ¡Pasión! we make our daiquiri with mango for its smooth texture, bright color, and tropical taste. To make the delectable pineapple chips I use as a garnish, you'll need a nonstick baking sheet, such as a Silpat. (See Special Ingredients and Tools.) You can use the sheet almost indefinitely for baking. Parchment paper won't work nearly as well.

SERVES 1

½ cup peeled and diced ripe, fragrant mango
¾ cup ice
1½ ounces light rum
1 ounce Simple Syrup
Pineapple chips (see recipe below) or thinly sliced
    mango, for garnish

■ In a blender jar, combine all the ingredients and blend until smooth. Pour into a martini glass, garnish with pineapple chips or mango slices, and serve.

SIMPLE SYRUP

MAKES 3 CUPS
2 cups sugar
2 cups water

■ In a medium saucepan, combine the sugar and water, stirring to moisten the sugar evenly with the water. Cook over low heat to dissolve the sugar. Raise the heat to moderate, shaking the pan often, and continue to cook until the mixture has formed a thick syrup, 5 to 10 minutes. Do not allow the sugar to caramelize or turn brown. Pour the syrup into a container and cool before using. Syrup may be made 1 week ahead and kept covered in the refrigerator.

PINEAPPLE CHIPS

MAKES ABOUT 40 CHIPS

1 firm but ripe golden pineapple, peeled and
    cut in half lengthwise
1 cup Simple Syrup

■ Line a baking pan with a Silpat sheet. Slice the pineapple as thinly and evenly as possible, using a mandoline, Benriner cutter, or deli slicer. One by one, dip the pineapple slices into the simple syrup, shaking off the excess. Arrange in a single layer on the baking sheet, close together but not touching. Place in a very low oven. (If using an electric oven, set at the lowest temperature, around 100°F. If using a gas oven, the pilot light alone should be warm enough.) Dry out overnight, or at least 8 hours. The pineapple chips should be crisp and dry. If desired, you can mold them into different shapes by working quickly while they're still warm. Store in a cookie tin at room temperature for up to 2 weeks.

Cocktails pictured clockwise from left: Watermelon Margarita; Mango Daiquiri; and Caipirinha ¡Pasión!.

Caipirinha ¡Pasión!

Caipirinha is a drink that is popular everywhere in Brazil, but especially at the beaches. It is based on cachaça, the potent white Brazilian liquor distilled from sugar cane. The two brands most frequently available in the United States are Cachaça 51 and Pitu. While a caipirinha always contains limes and sugar, at ¡Pasión! we use every tropical fruit from pineapple to passion fruit.

SERVES 1

½ lime, scrubbed and cut into 3 or 4 wedges
1 tablespoon sugar
1 ounce passion fruit purée
2½ ounces cachaça

■ Cut each lime wedge in half crosswise. Chill an 8-ounce rocks glass by swirling it with crushed ice, then discard the ice. Add the lime wedges and sugar to the glass. Using a wooden muddler or the back of a heavy spoon, crush the wedges with the sugar to release the fragrant oils from the rind. Add the passion fruit purée. Fill the glass with ice, pour in the cachaça, and serve.

Papi Sour

This cocktail is a favorite of my Cuban father-in-law, Enrique Menocal, and I've named it in his honor. The rye whiskey is authentically American, first distilled in Pennsylvania. Angostura bitters, now produced in Trinidad, originally came from Venezuela and were invented by a German doctor, Johann Siegert, who joined Simon Bolivar in the 1820s in his fight against the Spanish throne. Siegert studied the native tropical plants, searching for a natural cure for illnesses suffered by the soldiers. His Angostura bitters are still used today in cocktails like this, though more for their pleasing bitterness than any curative effects.

SERVES 1

1½ ounces rye whiskey
¾ ounce Simple Syrup (see recipe on page 168)
1¼ ounces fresh lime juice
1 ounce fresh orange juice
2 dashes Angostura bitters
Orange slices, for garnish

■ In an 8-ounce rocks glass filled with ice, combine the rye, simple syrup, lime juice, orange juice, and bitters. Shake vigorously, garnish with the orange slices, and serve.

Cocktails pictured clockwise from left: Sangrita; Tomatillo Bloody Mary with Pickled Okra; Papi Sour; tequila for serving with Sangrita.

Tomatillo Bloody Mary
with Pickled Okra

At ¡Pasión! we make even classic drinks like the Bloody Mary with our own twist. Here I use tart, refreshing tomatillos (Mexican husk tomatoes) instead of the traditional tomato, and I garnish the drink with my own pickled okra. The Bloody Mary originated in Paris in the 1920s when the bartender at Harry's New York Bar combined tomato juice with vodka. A patron named the drink after Mary, a woman whose acquaintance he had made at the Bucket of Blood Club in Chicago. Henry Avadia, our former bartender, who is originally from Colombia, invented the fabulous hot sauce we use for this drink. Try his recipe, opposite, or substitute Tabasco.

Start the savory pickled okra a week before you plan to serve it. It will keep well in the refrigerator for at least a month, as long as you remove it using a clean stainless-steel or wooden spoon—never your hands.

SERVES 1

4 fresh tomatillos, husked and chopped
Dash of lemon juice
Dash of lime juice
¼ teaspoon ground black pepper
1 teaspoon Worcestershire sauce
1 teaspoon Henry's Hot Sauce (see recipe, opposite)
    or Tabasco
½ teaspoon granulated garlic
2 teaspoons salt
1 tablespoon prepared horseradish
1½ ounces vodka
Pickled Okra, for garnish

■ In a blender jar, combine all the ingredients except the okra. Blend until the tomatillos are completely puréed. Serve in a 14-ounce highball glass filled with ice, and garnish with one pickled okra pod.

PICKLED OKRA
MAKES 2 CUPS

¾ cup extra virgin olive oil
1 pound fresh okra, stems trimmed
½ cup small diced onion
4 serrano chiles, halved lengthwise
8 bay leaves
1 teaspoon Mexican oregano
1 cup red wine vinegar
2 tablespoons sugar
1 tablespoon kosher salt

■ In a large, nonreactive skillet, warm ¼ cup of the olive oil over moderately high heat. Add the okra and sauté until lightly browned. Add the onion and cook for about 5 minutes, until soft but not brown. Add the chiles, bay leaves, oregano, vinegar, sugar, and salt, and bring to the boil. Turn off the heat, cool to room temperature, and spoon into a sterilized 16-ounce canning jar (see To Sterilize Jars for Escabeche on page 124). Cover with remaining ½ cup olive oil. Marinate for 1 week, covered and refrigerated, before using. Once you've removed okra from the jar, add more oil, if needed, to cover the remaining okra.

Henry's Hot Sauce

This chunky hot sauce is full of flavor. It's hot, naturally, but it has a complexity not normally found in bottled hot sauces because of all the different chiles. It will last indefinitely in your refrigerator. Try it in a Bloody Mary, on eggs, or on hamburgers for a memorable taste kick.

Makes about 1 quart

4 serrano chiles

1 jalapeño chile

3 habanero chiles

1 cup cachucha chiles (see Special Ingredients)

4 ripe plum tomatoes, quartered lengthwise

½ medium red onion, peeled and cut into pieces

3 tablespoons peeled garlic cloves

¼ large bunch cilantro, washed, including all stems

¼ large bunch Italian parsley, washed, including tender stems only

½ cup Crystal hot sauce

6 tablespoons Worcestershire sauce

¼ cup tomato juice

6 tablespoons extra virgin olive oil

2 tablespoons kosher salt

Trim the stems from all the chiles. Using a meat grinder fitted with the largest-hole grinder plate, or a food processor, grind the chiles. Add the tomatoes, onion, garlic, cilantro, and parsley and process to combine; if using a meat grinder, switch the grinder plate to one with smaller holes and grind again. Whisk in the Crystal hot sauce, Worcestershire, tomato juice, olive oil, and salt, and combine. Pour into a sterilized glass jar (see directions on page 124), cover tightly, and refrigerate for 1 week before using. The sauce will keep for at least 3 months in the refrigerator.

Mulata del Fuego

Named for the beautiful mulata *(mixed blood) women of the Dominican Republic, this drink combines dark and light rum for an enticing combination. While the garnish of edible tropical orchids is optional, I think these beautiful, long-lasting, magenta blossoms are the only proper tribute to the beauty of the mulatas. To order them, see Special Ingredients and Tools.*

SERVES 1

1 ounce dark rum

1 ounce light rum

½ ounce fresh lime juice

½ ounce Simple Syrup (see recipe on page 168)

Edible orchid, for garnish

■ In a cocktail shaker, combine both rums, lime juice, and simple syrup with ice. Shake well to chill, strain, and serve "up" in a martini glass. If available, float an edible orchid on top to garnish.

Presidente Menocal

This cocktail is named after General Mario García Menocal, who was Cuba's president from 1913 to 1921, and the great-great grandfather of my wife, Lucia Menocal. At the time the drink was invented, Americans subjected to Prohibition were invited to "Come to Cuba and bathe in Bacardi rum." Long one of Cuba's favorite cocktails, it was popular with American tourists who went to La Florida, a friendly dive near the docks, to drink one immediately upon arrival, and perhaps to glimpse Ernest Hemingway, who frequented the spot.

SERVES 1

1½ ounces white rum
½ ounce sweet red vermouth
3 dashes grenadine
3 dashes white Curaçao
Pineapple chunk and a maraschino cherry, for garnish

■ In a cocktail shaker, combine the rum, vermouth, grenadine, and Curacao with ice. Shake well to chill, strain, and serve "up" in a martini glass. Skewer the pineapple and maraschino cherry on a toothpick and use to garnish.

Rum Negroni with Sugar Cane Stick

The Negroni is a potent Italian cocktail made with Campari bitters, which were invented around 1850 by Gaspare Campari, who learned his trade as a licoriste, or master drink maker, in Turin, Italy. Many sources attribute the cocktail's name to Count Camillo Negroni, a Florentine aristocrat who ordered this drink in the numerous bars he frequented in the 1920s. At ¡Pasión! we substitute Caribbean dark rum for the usual gin. Although it's not traditional, the warm, rounded flavor of the rum complements the Campari and red vermouth beautifully, and our Negroni is just as beguiling as the original.

SERVES 1

1 ounce dark rum
1 ounce Campari
1 ounce sweet red vermouth
1 sugar cane stick (see instructions on page 90)

■ In a cocktail shaker, combine the rum, Campari, and vermouth with ice. Shake well to chill, strain, and serve "up" in a martini glass. Garnish with the sugar cane stick.

Cocktails pictured clockwise from left: Cuban Manhattan; Rum Negroni with Sugar Cane stick; Golden Banana Martini; and Mulata del Fuego.

Sangria Roja

Sangria, a mixture of macerated fruits, red wine, and brandy, was originally made in Spain with Rioja and other Spanish red wines. The name comes from the Spanish word for blood, sangre, *because of its color. Where I grew up, in Buenos Aires, Malbec was just about the only red wine we drank, and to me it makes the perfect sangria. Malbec grapes from Bordeaux were imported into Argentina more than one hundred years ago and became extremely well established. Argentinean Malbec combines a rich, weighty mouthfeel with a soft silkiness normally associated with lighter wines. If you can't find Malbec, substitute a Rioja "Vino de Crianza," meaning it has spent one year in a barrel and is at least three years old.*

SERVES 6

1 (750 ml) bottle Malbec red wine

2 limes, peeled and sliced

2 lemons, peeled and sliced

2 oranges, peeled and sliced

2 apples, peeled and sliced

2 ounces brandy

3 ounces Simple Syrup (see recipe on page 168)

8 ounces club soda

■ In a large glass jar or pitcher, combine the red wine, 1 lime, 1 lemon, 1 orange, 1 apple, and the brandy. Cover and macerate in the refrigerator for 24 hours. The next day, strain the liquid into a 2-quart serving pitcher filled with ice, discarding the fruit. Add the remaining lime, lemon, orange, and apple, the simple syrup, and the club soda. Stir well and serve in wineglasses, making sure that each glass includes a portion of the fruit.

White Wine and Peach Sangria

Sangria made with white wine is known as Sangria Blanco. Although Sangria was originally created with Spanish reds, it didn't take long for the producers of Cava, the Spanish sparkling wine, to come up with their own version. Once I sampled it in Spain, I enjoyed this summertime variation. I find that frozen peaches make a wonderful sangria, but of course I would garnish the drink with fresh peach slices when they're in season.

SERVES 6

1 (750 ml) bottle Cava (Spanish sparkling wine)

2 ounces peach schnapps

1 lime, peeled and sliced

1 cup frozen peach slices, or sliced firm but ripe peaches

8 ounces club soda

3 ounces Simple Syrup (see recipe on page 168)

3 large firm but ripe peaches, cut into thin slices, for garnish

■ In a large glass jar or pitcher, stir together the sparkling wine and schnapps. Add the lime and frozen peaches. Cover and refrigerate for about 2 hours. Strain the liquid into a 2-quart glass serving pitcher filled with ice, discarding the fruit. Add the club soda and simple syrup. Stir well and serve over ice in wineglasses garnished with the peach slices.

Cocktails pictured: White Wine and Peach Sangria in foreground; Sangria Roja in background.

Cuban Manhattan

At ¡Pasión! we make our Manhattan with dark rum instead of the original rye whiskey. The beautiful society hostess Jennie Jerome served the original cocktail at a banquet she hosted at New York's Manhattan Club in the early 1870s. In 1874, she married the British politician Lord Randolph Churchill and later gave birth to their son, Winston. Our Cuban Manhattan depends on the smooth and mellow premium rums originally developed by Don Facundo Bacardi Massó, who started the Barcardi Company in 1862.

SERVES 1

2½ ounces dark rum
½ ounce sweet red vermouth
2 drops Angostura bitters
Maraschino cherry, for garnish

■ In a cocktail shaker, combine the rum, vermouth, and bitters with ice. Shake well to chill, strain, and serve "up" in a martini glass. Garnish with the cherry.

Watermelon Margarita

One story about the origins of the Margarita cocktail credits an American, Margarita Samas, with inventing the drink at a poolside party at her Acapulco vacation house in 1948. Her friend Tommy Hilton, owner of the Hilton hotels, started serving it in his American hotel cocktail lounges. At ¡Pasión! we use the ultimate summer fruit, watermelon, to make a slushy semi-frozen Margarita. The firm, sweet, seedless watermelon called Sugar Baby makes the best margaritas. Use any good quality tequila labeled añejo, *which must be aged for a minimum of one year in white oak casks, or silver tequila, which is aged in wax-lined vats.*

SERVES 4

2 limes
¼ cup kosher salt (for glass rims)
5 cups diced watermelon, frozen for several hours
    until firm
6 ounces white tequila
3 tablespoons sugar
½ cup watermelon cubes, for garnish

■ Squeeze the juice from the limes. Rub the lime hulls around the rims of the cocktail glasses to moisten lightly. Place the salt in a saucer slightly larger than the rim of the glass. Invert the glasses, one at a time, onto the salt, twisting back and forth until the salt coats the rim evenly. Shake off the excess salt. (You'll have extra salt left in the saucer.) In a blender jar, combine the watermelon, tequila, and sugar, and purée until smooth. Pour into the prepared glasses and serve, garnished with watermelon cubes threaded on a toothpick.

Golden Banana Martini

As made by Professor Jerry Thomas, the famed bartender at the old Occidental Hotel in San Francisco who allegedly invented the cocktail for a gold miner on his way to the town of Martinez, the original martini called for gin, sweet vermouth, a dash of maraschino, bitters, a slice of lemon, and simple syrup. By 1900 the dry martini had come into fashion on both sides of the Atlantic. In recent years creative bartenders have come up with all sorts of variations. At ¡Pasión! we make this delightful martini with vanilla-infused vodka, banana liqueur, and aguardiente, the Spanish spirit popular in parts of Argentina.

SERVES 1

2 ounces Stolichnaya vanilla vodka
1 ounce banana liqueur
½ ounce aguardiente
3 to 4 thin slices firm but ripe banana, peeled or not
　　as desired

■ In a cocktail shaker, combine the vodka, banana liqueur, and aguardiente with ice. Shake well to chill, strain, and serve "up" in a martini glass. Garnish with banana slices.

Sangrita

Not to be confused with fruity sangria, this fiery red combination of citrus and chili sauce is the traditional chaser for tequila in Mexico, particularly in Oaxaca and Jalisco, where tequila originated. Literally "little bloody thing," sangrita is traditionally made with the juice of freshly squeezed sour oranges. As they're difficult to obtain here, we use a combination of lime and orange. Serve the sangrita as a chaser accompanied by shot glasses of the best quality aged (añejo) tequila. See Special Ingredients and Tools for sources for the tiny, super-hot whole chile pequin.

SERVES 4

2 pounds ripe red tomatoes, chopped
　　(about 6 tomatoes)
1 cup fresh orange juice
¼ cup fresh lime juice
¼ cup diced white onion
¼ teaspoon salt
½ to 1 teaspoon ground chile pequin, or 1 to 2 whole
　　chile pequin
Lime wedges

■ In a blender jar or food processor, combine the tomatoes, orange juice, lime juice, onion, and salt. Blend until smooth. Add the chile in small amounts until the sangrita is as hot as you like. To remove the tomato skins and seeds, strain through a food mill or sieve into a pitcher. Transfer the Sangrita to a pitcher, cover, and refrigerate for at least 1 hour before serving in small glasses, accompanied by shot glasses of tequila and the lime wedges.

BASIC RECIPES

Basic Braising Liquid

I braise many foods, including octopus and shrimp, in this flavorful liquid. That way, instead of the cooking liquid drawing flavor from the seafood, which is the goal when making a stock, you're imparting a subtle flavor to the seafood itself. Once the seafood has been poached, you may strain the liquid and either use it one more time for poaching or, especially if you've just poached shrimp or scallops rather than octopus, use it as the base for seafood chowder or soup.

MAKES 3 QUARTS

3 quarts cold water
2 tablespoons pickling spice
1 tablespoon hot red pepper flakes
¼ cup kosher salt
¼ cup Tabasco sauce
2 lemons, cut in half

■ In a large pot, combine the water, pickling spice, red pepper flakes, salt, Tabasco, the juice squeezed from the lemons, and the lemon halves. Bring to the boil; then reduce the heat to a simmer. Cook 10 minutes; then strain, discarding the solids. Use immediately to poach seafood, or cool to room temperature; then cover and refrigerate for up to 4 days before using. If desired, freeze for up to 1 month.

Basic Ceviche Marinade

I use this basic marinade for many types of ceviche. I like to vary it by substituting sour orange juice for the lime juice, or grapefruit or tangerine juice for the orange juice. When Meyer lemons are in season, I combine ½ cup of their juice with ¼ cup orange or tangerine juice. Depending on the flavor I'm trying to achieve, I might also add a little sugar, curry powder, chipotle chile powder, or cumin.

MAKES ABOUT ¾ CUP

½ cup fresh lime juice
¼ cup fresh orange juice
2 teaspoons kosher salt

■ In a medium nonreactive (stainless-steel or enameled) bowl, combine the lime juice, orange juice, and salt. Use to marinate seafood for ceviche from between 20 minutes (for very fresh, thinly sliced, mild fish) to 24 hours (for stronger-tasting seafood such as sea scallops).

Lobster Stock

It might seem excessive to make your own lobster stock just to prepare the Oyster Ceviche with Roasted Banana–Tamarindo Sauce, Tooloom Balls (see recipe on page 68). But if you want to experience that lively and unusual dish, there's no getting around it.

MAKES 1 CUP

2 whole cooked lobster carcasses, from about 4 pounds
    of whole lobsters, meat removed and reserved
    for another use
1 tablespoon vegetable oil
½ cup roughly chopped onion
½ cup roughly chopped carrot
½ cup roughly chopped celery (or ½ cup each celery
    and fennel)
2 tablespoons tomato purée
2 sprigs fresh thyme
1 bay leaf
Stems from ½ bunch Italian parsley

■ Preheat the oven to 350°F. Clean the lobsters, removing and discarding the stomach sac just behind the eyes. Cut up the shells, using heavy kitchen shears. Mix the chopped lobster shells with the oil. Spread out in a single layer on a large roasting pan. Roast about 30 minutes, until browned, and add the remaining ingredients. Roast 30 minutes longer, or until all ingredients are well browned but not charred.

■ Transfer the contents of the pan to a large stockpot. Cover with cold water by about 3 inches. Bring to the boil, skimming and discarding the white foam. Reduce the heat to a bare simmer, and cook 45 minutes, until the stock has a definite lobster flavor without an overcooked taste. Strain through a sieve or china cap, pressing well with the back of a ladle to extract all the liquid. Discard the solids.

■ Place the stock in a medium saucepan and reduce by three-quarters, until 1 cup of liquid remains.

Tomato Confit

There are many uses for these fabulous preserved toma-
toes. They are absolutely wonderful on a grilled cheese
sandwich, in an omelet, or topping a hamburger. They
are slowly baked at very low heat, drying for three days,
concentrating their flavor and eliminating the excess
water. However, that means you'll need to leave your
oven on for all that time.

As long as they're covered with the olive oil, the
tomatoes will keep in the refrigerator for at least a
month. To avoid any bacteria growth, use a clean fork,
rather than your hands, to fish out the tomatoes.

MAKES 1½ POUNDS CONFIT

5 pounds plum tomatoes
1 cup whole garlic cloves
4 sprigs of basil on the branch
2 cups extra virgin olive oil
2 tablespoons kosher salt

■ Bring a large pot of water to the boil. Add all the tomatoes (if your pot is smaller, do this in 2 batches) and bring
the water back to the boil. Fill a large bowl with ice and
water. Using a wire skimmer, scoop out the tomatoes
and place in the ice water to stop the cooking. (To tell
when the tomatoes are done, chill one in the water and
then check; if the skin slips off easily, they're ready.)

■ Peel the tomatoes and discard the skins. Cut the
peeled tomatoes in half through the stem end. Using
your fingers, scoop out the seeds and either discard or
reserve for making stock.

■ Combine the peeled tomatoes with the garlic, basil,
olive oil, and salt. Spread out evenly in a baking pan and
place in the oven. Heat the oven to 150°F and cook the
tomatoes slowly for 2 days. Reduce the temperature to
100°F and bake for 1 day longer, until the tomatoes are
shriveled and slightly darkened in color. Use in a recipe
or transfer to a container, cover, and refrigerate for up
to 1 month.

Annatto Oil

The small, hard annatto seed, also called achiote, is sold both whole and ground. It is prized in Hispanic cuisine for its slightly bitter, earthy flavor and distinctive color. Annatto seeds are dark russet-red and extremely hard. They are available at Latino markets and from specialty spice companies. They are used throughout the Caribbean and Latin America to make a delicately flavored red oil. In this recipe, it's important to use a thermometer (one of the most useful of kitchen tools) to ensure that the oil is heated only to 108°F. Otherwise it will lose its color and turn brown rather than brilliant red.

MAKES 2 CUPS OIL

2 cups mild vegetable oil (such as soy or canola)
1 tablespoon annatto seeds

■ Place oil and seeds in a small, heavy pan and heat gently to 108°F only. Remove from the heat and allow the mixture to steep for 30 minutes; then strain the oil and discard the seeds. Cover and keep the oil in a cool, dark place for up to 2 months.

Slow-Roasted Garlic and Garlic Oil

One of the best things to happen to garlic lovers is the advent of high-quality, pre-peeled garlic. While I don't find it to be quite as oil-rich and fresh tasting as hand-peeled garlic, it's a far sight better than using the bottled, chopped garlic that tastes old and bitter and contains preservatives.

Initially, pre-peeled garlic was only available to chefs in 5-pound plastic containers, but recently I've seen a 1-pound container in the supermarket produce department. Be sure to check the cloves inside the container. They should be creamy in color, with no whitish mold on the outside and little to no surface wrinkling. If the stem end is prominent and woody, I remove it by slicing off a thin piece from the end. With a container of this peeled garlic (I recommend Christopher Ranch brand from California), it's a breeze to make versatile slow-roasted garlic cloves. The oil in which the garlic is cooked is just as versatile in its own right. I like to use it for sautéing and in dressings.

MAKES 2 CUPS

1 (1-pound) container peeled garlic cloves
2 cups mild vegetable oil, or 1 cup each vegetable oil
   and olive oil
½ cup water
2 teaspoons kosher salt
½ teaspoon freshly ground black pepper

■ Preheat the oven to 300°F. Place the garlic, oil, water, salt, and pepper in a baking dish with a lid. Cover and bake for 45 minutes. The oil should be gently bubbling. Remove from the oven and cool. Refrigerate in a covered container for up to 1 month.

Poached Octopus

Here I use a large whole octopus, which I buy already cleaned and usually frozen. While the Spanish cook their octopus for as long as two hours, I prefer a chewier texture, so I cook it for only about half an hour. If you like your octopus more tender, cook it for at least an hour, or until it is tender enough for your taste. Some chefs like to peel off the rather gelatinous outer skin. I leave it on, because I like the texture.

3 quarts cold water
1 cup coarsely chopped carrots
1 cup coarsely chopped celery
1 cup coarsely chopped onion
2 cups dry white wine (or dry
    white vermouth)
2 tablespoons dried oregano
2 teaspoons dried thyme
2 tablespoons kosher salt
1 tablespoon whole black
    peppercorns
1 large octopus, about 8 pounds,
    defrosted if frozen

■ In a large pot, bring the water, carrots, celery, onion, wine, oregano, thyme, salt, and peppercorns to the boil. Simmer 15 minutes; then add the octopus and bring the liquid back to the boil. Reduce the heat to a bare simmer and cook very slowly for about 30 minutes, or until the octopus is firm yet tender when pierced with a fork. Turn off the heat and allow the octopus to cool in its cooking liquid. When ready to serve, drain and discard the cooking liquid.

Cooking Lobsters

If you use female lobsters, you'll have the added bonus of eating the colorful and delicious coral, or lobster roe. Ask your fishmonger to help you choose female lobsters. The female will have a short, wide tail rather than the longer, skinnier tail of the male. Turn the lobster over and look at its feelers. The first set, closest to the head, will be soft on a female and hard on a male.

1 to 2 (1½-pound) live lobsters
1 quart Basic Braising Liquid for each lobster
    (see recipe on page 182)

■ Hold the lobster with your hand on top of the body portion. The claws should be enclosed in rubber bands, but even if they're not, the lobster can't move its claws backward. Find the spot where the head shell connects to the main thorax, or body, shell. Stab the point of a heavy chef's knife into the lobster shell. This will kill the lobster immediately.

■ To keep the lobster meat from curling while it cooks, stick a long bamboo or metal skewer through the body, from just in front of the fan-shaped tail shell to the thorax section on the underside of the body. This step is not absolutely necessary if you'd prefer to skip it.

■ Drop the lobsters into the boiling liquid, cover, and cook 4 minutes, stirring once. The lobsters should be bright red with lightly curled tail shells. (If the tail has not been skewered, it will begin to curl up when the lobster is ready.) Remove lobsters from the pot and place in a large bowl of ice mixed with water. Strain and reserve the Basic Braising Liquid. Cool to room temperature and freeze for use another time.

Slow-Roasted Beets

Gently roasted beets are a delicious and versatile addition to your repertoire, both for their brilliant color and their sweet flavor. They take very well to all sorts of marinades and maintain their flavor for at least a week after cooking. My favorites are the large, fresh-picked, magenta-colored Texas beets that are sold with their tops. (Cook the tops separately as you would spinach or chard.) Choose beets that are evenly sized with tight skin that feels hard, and avoid any that are wrinkled and soft to the touch.

MAKES 1 POUND

2 bunches large beets with their tops removed and
    reserved for another use
2 tablespoons olive oil
2 teaspoons kosher salt
½ teaspoon freshly ground black pepper

■ Preheat the oven to 300°F. Wash the beets, scrubbing them with an abrasive pad if they feel sandy. Rub dry. Rub the beets with the olive oil, then the salt and pepper. Arrange the beets on a wire rack over a baking pan. Roast 2 hours, or until soft when stuck with a skewer. Remove from the oven, cool to room temperature, and slip off their skins. (It's easiest to do this when the beets are cool enough to handle but not cold.) Place in a zipper-lock plastic bag and refrigerate until needed, or marinate immediately.

Note: When cutting off the beet tops, be sure to leave on about ½ inch of stalk. If you cut into the flesh of the beet itself, it will bleed.

Natural Green Coloring (Chlorophyll)

No other common plant produces such a strong, concentrated green color as does spinach. Use this natural green coloring in small amounts to add bright color to the Lime Allioli.

MAKES ABOUT ¼ CUP COLORING

1 (10-ounce) bag fresh spinach, stems discarded
1 cup water

■ Purée the spinach with the water in a blender. Strain to remove the pulp, or press through a vegetable juicer and discard the pulp. In a small pan, gently heat the raw spinach juice until the green matter (or chlorophyll) coagulates; then remove from heat. Allow the heavier green matter to settle; then pour off and discard the clear liquid, reserving the green solids. Cover and refrigerate this chlorophyll to use as needed. It keeps at least 3 days.

Seafood Safety
in Detail

Purchase only the highest quality, or sushi-grade, seafood for ceviche.

Always buy fish and seafood from reputable establishments that have high standards for quality and sanitation. The fishmonger's counter should smell briny and fresh. The fish should look almost alive, with clear eyes, shiny flesh, and bright red gills. It costs more to maintain a high-quality fish-and-seafood operation, so avoid buying any so-called bargains. The muscle of a whole fish, the part usually eaten, doesn't normally carry bacteria and viruses. However, improper handling can contaminate steaks and fish fillets.

Keep seafood extra cold at all times.

To prevent growth of bacteria, keep fish and other seafood that is not alive as close to a temperature of 32°F or below as possible. Get purchased seafood home quickly; ask your fishmonger for a plastic bag filled with crushed ice to keep the seafood cold, especially in hot weather, and immediately transfer it to the refrigerator when you get home. Wrap fresh fish in plastic wrap; then place in zipper-lock bags or airtight containers. Store it in the coldest part of the refrigerator—in the meat or vegetable compartment or on open shelves close to the back.

To maintain it in the best condition, pack wrapped seafood inside a container filled with crushed ice or surround with frozen "blue ice" packs.

Before preparing ceviche, inspect and then freeze fish that may carry parasites.

Parasites such as tapeworms, flatworms, and roundworms occur naturally in some fish. They are another potential safety concern when eating raw fish. Fortunately, parasitic infections from ocean fish are rare in the United States, and there has been no significant increase due to the growing popularity of raw fish dishes. Reputable seafood packinghouses inspect fish by candling (holding them under light to search for parasites), and highly skilled sushi chefs are trained to detect and remove parasites. The parasite is a tightly coiled, clear worm, ½- to ¾-inch long, that imbeds itself in the flesh. At home, you can inspect your fish by holding each fillet up before a light so that any parasites can be seen and removed.

There are two main types of parasites to be concerned about. Roundworms are found in saltwater fish such as cod, plaice, halibut, rockfish, herring, pollock, sea bass, and flounder. Fish tapeworms may be found in freshwater fish such as pike and perch, as well as anadromous (freshwater and saltwater) fish such as salmon. While wild salmon often carry roundworm larvae in their flesh, farm-raised salmon—most of the salmon we eat—are free of parasites.

Pelagic fish such as tuna probably have the least amount of parasites because of their wide-roaming migrations. Tuna, near the top of the food chain, may consume prey that have parasites, but they generally don't remain in an area long enough to ingest a great deal. However, there are reports of humans becoming infected with roundworms after ingesting raw yellowfin tuna. Fish that don't move around much are more likely to have parasites. Juvenile or smaller fish have had less time in which to have become infected with parasites, and fish that grow quickly also have less time to pick up parasites.

To be extra careful, freeze fish intended to be eaten raw long enough to kill any existing parasites.

The Food and Drug Administration advises freezing fish long enough to kill any parasites. However, many sushi chefs and ceviche cooks don't like to freeze fish because it does affect the texture and juiciness of the final product. At home, you may want to freeze to an internal temperature of -4°F for seven days, or -3°F internal temperature for fifteen hours. In a home freezer at 0°F to 10°F, it can take up to five days to kill all the parasites, especially in large fish. While dead parasites are not harmful when ingested, they are certainly unappealing. If the fish contains visible parasites, you may remove them by hand before preparing the fish for ceviche. In commercial operations where freezing temperatures are much colder, a temperature of -40°F kills any parasites within fifteen hours.

Note that cold-smoked seafood may not be safe to eat unless it has been properly frozen first. Unlike hot smoking, cold smoking does not use heat, and the fish doesn't reach the temperature required to kill the parasites.

Keep "live" shellfish alive with ventilation and moderately cold temperature.

Refrigerate live clams, oysters, mussels, crabs, lobsters, and crayfish in well-ventilated containers in a not-too-cold part of the refrigerator. Temperatures too low can kill them. Cover the container with a damp cloth or paper towel rather than sealing it airtight; they'll live longer with air circulation. Storing live shellfish in salt water shortens their shelf life, and storing in fresh water kills them.

Clean shellfish well.

Rinse or scrub shellfish as necessary to remove dirt or debris, but avoid soaking for long periods of time in fresh water. Wash your hands with warm, soapy water before and after preparing and serving shellfish.

Avoid cross-contamination when handling seafood.

Store raw seafood in leak-proof containers or bags. Prevent it from dripping or splashing onto other foods and from being contaminated by other foods. Handle and store raw seafood and cooked seafood separately. It's especially important that you prevent raw seafood from touching or dripping or splashing onto foods that won't be cooked before being eaten, such as salad greens or fruit. Don't transfer bacteria from one food or food-contact surface (your hands, utensils, knives, cutting boards) to another when handling, storing, or preparing seafood. Thoroughly wash your hands, utensils, containers, and any food-preparation surfaces after touching or preparing raw seafood.

Thaw seafood in a cold environment.

Place frozen seafood immediately in the freezer when you bring it home. Store in the original moisture- and vapor-proof package. Frozen seafood packaged in over-wrapped trays should be repackaged in plastic wrap, freezer paper, or other moisture- and vapor-proof material before storing in the freezer. Keep seafood frozen rock-hard at 0°F or below until ready to use.

For best quality and safety, thaw frozen seafood slowly in the refrigerator overnight. Never thaw seafood in warm or standing water or at room temperature, for these environments encourage bacteria to grow. Thinner parts of frozen seafood thaw faster than thicker parts, and the outer edges may start to spoil before the center has thawed. The rule is: Freeze it quickly and thaw it slowly.

Always buy clams, oysters, and mussels from a licensed, reputable dealer.

Bivalve mollusks, such as clams and oysters, are commonly eaten raw or partially cooked. Because bivalves live in areas close to the shore, they are vulnerable to bacteria and viruses from human and land-animal sources carried into coastal waters. These shellfish, which obtain food by pumping water through their digestive systems and filtering out small organisms, may collect bacteria and viruses in the process.

People can ingest these organisms when they eat these foods raw. Thus, health risks from mollusks are usually directly related to the quality of the water from which they have been harvested. Because mollusks must be harvested from certified waters and meet safety standards, large numbers of raw clams and oysters are eaten each year without any problem. Still, some shellfish-related illnesses occur. Many reported illnesses are believed to be the result of "bootlegging," or the illegal harvesting of shellfish from uncertified waters. To be sure your clams and oysters are safe, buy only from reputable dealers.

If your immune system is compromised, avoid eating all raw mollusks.

Bacteria of the Vibrio family, natural summertime inhabitants of clean (unpolluted) coastal waters, can result in other illnesses. When they are in season, these bacteria can accumulate in mollusks. Although the bacteria do not affect the health of the shellfish, they can cause illness in people eating raw or undercooked bivalves. Anyone with a compromised immune system is considered "at risk" for contracting Vibrio infections. These infections cause death in almost half the people who contract them, so they need to be taken very seriously.

Never eat dead shellfish.

Never eat shellfish such as clams, oysters, mussels, crabs, lobsters, and crayfish that have died. Live clams, oysters, and mussels have tightly closed shells, or shells that will close when tapped. Discard any clams or mussels with broken or gaping shells. Mussels, especially, have thin, easily shattered shells. Live crabs, lobsters, and crayfish move their legs. Dead shellfish spoil rapidly and develop off-flavor and off-odors. Soft-shell clams can't completely close their shells but should move when touched.

When cooking seafood, cook to proper temperature to ensure safety.

Cook seafood to an internal tempera-ture of at least 145°F. Though cooking to 160°F or higher is recommended to kill all bacteria, high temperatures can easily cause seafood to be overcooked and to become dry and tough. Properly cooked fish should be opaque and moist and should flake easily.

Cool cooked seafood as rapidly as possible.

When preparing large amounts of cooked seafood (such as a large pot of clam chowder, or the mussel escabeche in this book), cool as quickly as possible. Transfer the cooked seafood to a clean container—prefer-ably metal, which is a good conductor. Place the container in your sink and surround it with a combination of ice and water (or add several frozen packs of "blue ice" to the water). Once the ice melts, drain some water away and add more ice to speed the process. Once the food is cool to the touch, refrigerate. If you place food that is still hot in your refrigerator, all the foods inside will warm up and your refrigerator will have to work hard to bring down the temperature, creating frost and potentially unsafe food spoilage conditions.

Avoid fish that carry naturally occurring toxins.

Toxins produced by naturally occurring marine algae can accumulate in fish and shellfish that inhabit the same marine environment. Unlike with bacteria and parasites, cooking does not destroy tox-ins. To reduce potential health risks, pur-chase seafood from reputable sources and use caution when eating fish or shellfish caught in unknown waters.

The marine toxin ciguatoxin can accumulate in some tropical saltwater reef fish, and poisoning can occur when those fish are eaten. Because the waters are monitored and tested, commercial fisheries are generally able to avoid areas that contain ciguatoxic fish. Individuals who harvest their own shellfish should check with local authorities and heed all warnings regarding shellfish-harvesting restrictions.

Escolar, puffer fish, and whelk may contain naturally occurring toxins. Escolar (*Lepidocybium flavobrunneum* and *Ruvettus pretiosus*) contains strong purgative oil that may cause illness. Puffer fish—the renowned Japanese delicacy, *fugu*—which may contain tetrodotoxin, may not be imported except under strict certifica-tion requirements and specific authori-zation from the FDA. Poisonings from tetrodotoxin have usually been associ-ated with the consumption of puffer fish from the Indo-Pacific oceans. Tetramine, a toxin found in the glands of a type of whelk, *Neptunia*, can be controlled by removing the glands.

Histamine or scombrotoxin poison-ing is caused by improper fish handling rather than by naturally occurring marine algae. Histamine can be rapidly produced when oily fish such as tuna, mackerel, bluefish, mahi-mahi, and amberjack are allowed to remain on the deck of a fishing boat or a dock for long periods in warm weather and begin to spoil. Histamine can cause an allergic-like reaction when the fish is eaten. Although it isn't usually severe, it can make the affected person quite uncomfortable.

Be aware of risk from chemical contaminants.

While the potential health risks from chemical contaminants like PCBs, mercury, and pesticides in fish have been difficult to quantify, levels in most commercial species are well below established limits. Large predatory fish that live for a long time, such as swordfish, can accumulate higher levels of contaminants such as mercury. These species are tested more frequently to ensure that the commercial supply meets government standards.

To minimize risk, eat a variety of fish and shellfish. Avoid eating excessive amounts of any single type of fish or shellfish. Avoid eating the internal organs of fish, the tomalley of lobsters, and the mustard of crabs, which can contain significantly higher amounts of contaminants than the flesh. Keep in mind that such ocean species as tuna, which spend their entire lives far from the shore, are less likely to contain contaminants than those that stay in shoreline areas.

Women who may become pregnant or are already pregnant should eat shark or swordfish no more than once a month. Other people should limit eating these fish to no more than once a week. Avoid eating fish or shellfish harvested by nonprofessionals for their personal consumption, because the seafood may come from contaminated waters.

Be sensitive to seafood allergies.

Seafood allergies have been estimated at less than $\frac{1}{10}$ of one percent of the population. These allergies are abnormal responses of the body's immune system to certain foods. A protein in the offending food "fools" the immune system into recognizing the food as a foreign invader. The immune system then produces antibodies to help fight the "invasion." Antibodies bind with other cells and release histamines. Histamines are responsible for allergy symptoms, which can affect the gastrointestinal tract, skin, and/or respiratory system.

Most allergies are specific to a certain species or type of seafood. For instance, someone who is allergic to fin fish may not be allergic to shellfish, and vice versa. However, if you know you are allergic to a certain type of seafood, question restaurant staff carefully before eating food you suspect contains a potential allergen, and carefully read ingredient listings on food labels. Sometimes even very small amounts of the allergen can trigger a reaction.

People who already have asthma may be more likely to have food allergies. Although allergic reactions are usually mild, some individuals can experience severe symptoms, such as anaphylactic shock, which can cause death. Allergies to seafood don't usually go away or diminish with age. In fact, allergic reactions may become more severe with each subsequent exposure to the offending food. That's why it's important to recognize an allergy or to have it diagnosed by a doctor. The allergy is managed by avoiding the offending food. There is no cure for food allergies. Anyone with a history of anaphylactic reactions should carry medication such as epinephrine and know how to self-administer it.

Special Ingredients and Tools

You can find virtually all of the special ingredients and kitchenware I call for at Hispanic, Asian, and international grocery stores in cities around the United States. More and more supermarkets are carrying exotic produce and interesting foreign foods. Here are a few sources for mail-order and online shopping.

Amazonas Imports, Inc.
10817 Sherman Way
Sun Valley, CA 91352
Phone: 818-982-1377
Fax: 818-982-3898
www.amazonasnaturalfoods.com
Rocoto chile, panca chile, amarillo chile, Huacatay black mint, cascabel, pasilla, serrano, pequin, guajillo, and chipotle chiles, cancha corn, and other foods from Latin America.

Art Culinaire
40 Mills Street
Morristown, NJ 07960
Phone: 973-993-5500/ 1-800-SO-TASTY
Fax: 973-993-8779
www.getartc.com
This international magazine for professional chefs sells Austrian pumpkin seed oil through its website.

Chile Today, Hot Tamale
2-D Great Meadow Lane
East Hanover, NJ 07936
Phone: 1-800-HOT-PEPPER
Fax: 973-884-4118
www.chiletoday.com
Guajillo, cascabel, ancho, chipotle, African bird peppers, and other fresh and dried chiles.

El Marketcito
3434 SW 171st Terrace
Miramar, FL 33027
Phone: 954-443-4372
Fax: 305-828-5226
www.elmarketcito.com
This online Latin supermarket carries tostoneros, cotija cheese, plantain cutters, tasajo, canned huitlacoche, and other foods from Latin America.

Florida Farms
Ron Burns
1345 Bay Lake Loup
Groveland, FL 347736
Phone: 352-429-4048
Fresh huitlacoche.

Importfood.com
PO Box 2054
Issaquah, WA 98027
Phone: 425-392-7516
Fax: 425-391-5658
www.importfood.com
Fresh kaffir lime leaves and other Thai specialty foods.

Indian Rock Produce
539 California Road
Quakertown, PA
Phone: 1-800-882-0512
Fresh sugar cane, passion fruit, culantro, kaffir lime leaves, and other unusual produce and herbs.

J. B. Prince Company
36 East 31st Street
New York, NY 10016-6821
Phone: 800-473-0577
Fax: 212-683-4488
www.jbprince.com
Metal and plastic ring molds, French mandolines, Japanese Benriner cutters.

Kitchen Market
218 8th Avenue
New York, NY 10011
Phone/fax: 1-888-468-4433
www.kitchenmarket.com
Ancho and amarillo chiles, annatto seeds, aji panco, canned huitlacoche, and other Latin foods.

Melissa's World of Produce
Phone: 800-588-0151
www.melissas.com
All sorts of unusual produce, including meyer lemons when in season.

New York Mutual Trading
25 Knickerbocker Rd.
Moonachie, NJ 07074
Phone: 201-933-9555, 212-564-4094
Fax: 201-933-7791
Asian tableware.

Previn Inc.
2044 Rittenhouse Street
Philadelphia, PA 19103
215-985-1996
Metal and plastic ring molds, French
mandolines, Japanese Benriner cutters.

Qzina
83 Myer Street
Hackensack, NJ 07601
Phone: 201-996-1939
www.Qzina.com
This online gourmet market carries
passion fruit and blood orange purées.

The Abalone Farm
PO Box 136
Cayucos, CA 93430
Phone: 877-367-2271
Fax: 805-995-0236
www.abalonefarm.com
Live abalone.

Uwajimaya
4601 6th Avenue South
Seattle, WA 98108
Phone: 800-889-1928
www.uwajimaya.com
Unagi, wasabi, sambal oelek, and
other Asian foods.

Glossary

AGUARDIENTE: A white, non-aged cane sugar liquor often flavored with anise seeds. Different versions of this potent spirit are produced throughout Central and South America.

AJI PANCA: *Aji* is the Peruvian word for a mild, fruity chile. Aji panca is available in jars in paste form. In Mexico and the Caribbean, it is known as *chile rojo seco* (dried red chile).

ALLIOLI: A mayonnaise-like sauce flavored with citrus juice, popular in Spain's Mediterranean coastal region. It is related to aioli, the beloved garlic mayonnaise of Provence.

AMARILLO CHILE: Deep golden yellow chile pepper native to Chile and used extensively in Peru. *Amarillo* is Spanish for "yellow."

ANCHO CHILE: Small, mild, dried poblano chile with a sweet plum-raisin flavor. It is available whole or as a chile powder.

ANGULAS: Tiny, almost transparent baby eels that are extremely popular as a tapas in Spain.

ANNATTO: Dark russet-red spice, mild in flavor, and extremely hard. The Mexican name, *achiote*, is also the name for a seasoning paste made from the crushed seeds with other spices and herbs. Annatto is prized in Hispanic cuisines for its slightly bitter, earthy flavor, and distinctive color.

BONIATO: This tropical sweet potato (also known as *batata, camote,* or Cuban sweet potato), is a member of the morning glory family. It resembles a cross between a baking potato and a sweet potato, with patchy pink to burgundy skin and creamy white flesh.

BOQUERONES: Spanish name for fresh white anchovies, cured in olive oil. They are popular at Spanish tapas bars and throughout Spain and South America.

BOTTARGA: Italian name for pressed, dried tuna roe or caviar. This salty, strongly flavored condiment is also sold under the French name *poutarge.*

CALABAZA: Also known as West Indian pumpkin, this large, firm, hard-skinned squash ranges in color from green to beige to light red-orange. Calabazas are extremely popular throughout the Caribbean, Central America, and South America. They have a sweet flavor, similar to that of butternut squash, with a firm texture and excellent keeping qualities.

CACHUCHA CHILE: Also known as *rocatillo*, this small green chile has a bonnet shape like that of the fiery habanero or Scotch bonnet pepper, but it is relatively mild in heat.

CANCHA: A Peruvian variety of starchy field corn kernels that have been dried.

CANELA: True cinnamon, also known as soft-stick or Mexican cinnamon. It is softer in texture than the familiar hard, pungent cinnamon sticks, with a paler color and mild flavor.

CASCABEL CHILE: Round, mild dried chile with rich, nutty flavor. *Cascabel* means "jingling bells," in reference to the rattling sound of the seeds in the dried pepper pod.

CHAYOTE: This squash goes by many regional names, including vegetable pear, *mirliton*, and *christophene.* Chayote is firm, shaped like a plump pear, and light green in color.

CHILE DE ARBOL: This chile gets its name from the Spanish word for a small tree, because of its slim, tapered shape. In Mexico, it is called "bird's beak" or "rat's tail." Small and extremely hot, it is used both fresh and dried.

CHILE PEQUIN: Also called *chiltepe*, this tiny, oval, dried chile is powerfully hot, with a rich flavor.

CHIPOTLE CHILE: Smoked jalapeño available dried, as chile powder, or in *adobo* (canned in a light marinade). Chipotles are very hot, with a distinct flavor.

COTIJA CHEESE: Dry, strongly flavored, firm cheese usually made with cow's milk. In Latino cooking, it is used as a garnish for refried beans or to enhance the flavor of other savory dishes.

CROQUETA: Spanish for "croquette." Served as a side dish or snack, *croquetas* are made from thick cream sauce or similar binder combined with finely chopped cooked meat, fish, cheese, or other ingredients. The mixture is usually formed into cylinders, then breaded and fried.

CUZCO CORN: A variety of corn native to Peru. Also called *cancha*, it is toasted or cooked before eating.

DAIKON RADISH: Traditional Japanese vegetable often found in Asian markets. Also called Japanese or giant white radish, it is typically grated or pickled and used as a garnish.

ESCABECHE: Spanish technique for flavoring and preserving cooked vegetables, fish, or meat, similar to pickling. After cooking, the ingredients are marinated in a vinegar-based liquid for several days, or as long as several weeks, allowing the flavors to blend and mellow.

GUAJILLO CHILE: Elongated, dark brownish red dried chile that is moderately spicy, with distinctive flavor. *Guajillo* is Spanish for "little gourd."

HAMACHI: Japanese name for yellowtail, a rich, flavorful fish in the large tuna-bonito family native to Pacific waters.

HOKKIGAI: Japanese name for Arctic surf clams with bright red tips. Triangular in shape, they are often served at sushi bars.

HUACATAY MINT: This herb from the Peruvian rain forest is a member of the marigold family. It is used as a seasoning, most commonly in purée form, and is similar in texture to pesto.

HUITLACOCHE: Considered a delicacy in Mexican cuisine, this edible fungus grows inside corn kernels. It is purple-black in color, with an earthy, slightly sweet flavor reminiscent of truffles.

KAFFIR LIME LEAVES: The glossy, dark leaves of the kaffir lime tree, usually imported from Southeast Asia or Hawaii, are used to impart a sweet, citric perfume to many cooked foods.

KA-SUMI: Japanese word for squid ink, usually sold frozen. It imparts a dramatic black color and mild briny flavor to marinades.

MALAGUETA PEPPER: Small, red, extremely hot chile with fruity overtones, also known as the African bird pepper because it is shaped like a bird's beak. It must be handled carefully to avoid irritating the skin.

MALANGA: The Spanish word for taro, a starchy root vegetable with lavender threads running through its white flesh. A single root can weigh as much as five pounds. The tough outer skin must be peeled before cooking.

MEXICAN OREGANO: Also known as Mexican sage, this is a different variety than the more familiar Mediterranean oregano. It is stronger, more minty, and less sweet, well suited to the spicy dishes of Mexico and Central America.

MIRASOL CHILE: Used fresh or dried, this chile takes its name from the habit of growing upward and "looking into the sun" *(mira sol)*. Its flavor is earthy, with faint plum and raisin overtones.

MIRIN: Sweet Japanese rice wine used only for cooking.

MOJO: This tangy sauce of citrus juice, oil, garlic, and other flavors (called *molho* in Brazilian Portuguese) is served as a condiment with cooked foods.

NANAMI TOGARASHI: Japanese chile and spice mix, containing hot chile powder, dried orange peel, sesame seeds, seaweed, and other spices.

NOPALES: Also known by the diminutive form *nopalitos,* the fleshy oval paddles of the nopal, or prickly pear cactus, have a flavor most reminiscent of bell peppers or okra. They are popular in Mexican and other Latin American cuisines.

PEPITAS: Edible pumpkin seeds, flat and green when raw, rounded and brownish green when toasted. In Latin American cuisines, they are often ground and used in sauces.

PEPPERCRESS: A peppery green related to watercress, with small, curled leaves that resemble a cross between curly parsley and chervil.

PICADILLO: A mixture of meat with aromatics like onion and garlic, and the bold flavors of cumin and sherry vinegar. It may include raisin, currants, olives, toasted almonds, or pine nuts. The word comes from the Spanish verb *picar,* to cut into small pieces.

PLANTAIN: A large, starchy variety of banana, called *platano* when green or unripe, *pinto* or *pinton* (painted) when half-ripe, and *maduro* when fully ripe, with black-spotted, yellow skin. Plantains are always cooked before eating.

POMELO: A large, thick-skinned citrus fruit, the precursor of the modern grapefruit. Also known as Thai grapefruit, it is available at Asian groceries and produce markets.

PUMPKIN SEED OIL: Favored by chefs for its deep, nutty flavor, this dark green oil made from roasted pumpkin seeds is best used uncooked, in salads, sauces, and vinaigrettes. The best comes from the Austrian Tyrol, where special varieties of pumpkin are raised for their seed.

ROCOTO CHILE: Spicy-hot chile popular in Peru. In Mexico, it is also called *chile manzano.* It is medium in size, rounded, and plump, with a characteristic heart shape. Rocoto is sold in jars, whole, or in purée form.

TAMARINDO: Also called Indian date, *tamarindo* is Spanish for the large fruit pod of a tamarind tree. The sour, prune-flavored pulp surrounding the seeds is widely used as a tart flavoring in South and Central America. It is available in dried and liquid form.

TASAJO: Dried salted beef (also called *carne seca,* Spanish for "dried meat") used in cooked dishes. Popular in Central and South America, it is similar to Cajun tasso ham.

TIRADITOS: Spanish for "ribbons" or "strips," *tiraditos* also refers to long, thin strips of raw fish, lightly marinated and served as a type of ceviche inspired by Japanese sashimi.

TOBIKO WASABI: Tobiko is Japanese flying fish roe. Mildly briny, it usually has a reddish tint. Tobiko wasabi is colored pale green with wasabi and has wasabi's characteristic horseradish-like bite.

TOSTONES: Pieces of starchy, unripe plantain that have been cooked, flattened, and then fried. Tostones may be flattened by hand or with a special press called a tostonero. They are usually served as a side dish.

WASABI: The wasabi plant, indigenous to Japan, is one of the rarest and most difficult to grow. Highly valued in Japanese cuisine for its hot horseradish-like taste, wasabi is available primarily in dried, powdered form, to be reconstituted and served as a condiment for seafood.

YUCA: Spanish word for the cassava or manioc root. It has hard white flesh that softens with cooking, similar to that of a potato, and is a popular starch in Central and South America.

XTABENTUM: A potent liqueur made with anise and honey, produced in the Yucatán region of Mexico.

For Our International Readers
Conversion Tables

Generic Formulas for Metric Conversion

Ounces to grams...................	multiply ounces by 28.35
Pounds to grams...................	multiply pounds by 453.5
Cups to liters.......................	multiply cups by .24
Fahrenheit to Centigrade.......	subtract 32 from Fahrenheit, multiply by 5 and divide by 9

Metric Equivalents for Volume

U.S.	Imperial	Metric	
1/8 tsp.	—	.6 mL	
1/2 tsp.	—	2.5 mL	
3/4 tsp.	—	4.0 mL	
1 tsp.	—	5.0 mL	
1 1/2 tsp.	—	7.0 mL	
2 tsp.	—	10.0 mL	
3 tsp.	—	15.0 mL	
4 tsp.	—	20.0 mL	
1 Tbsp.	—	15.0 mL	
1 1/2 Tbsp.	—	22.0 mL	
2 Tbsp. (1/8 cup)	1 fl. oz	30.0 mL	
2 1/2 Tbsp.	—	37.0 mL	
3 Tbsp.	—	44.0 mL	
1/3 cup	—	57.0 mL	
4 Tbsp. (1/4 cup)	2 fl. oz	59.0 mL	
5 Tbsp.	—	74.0 mL	
6 Tbsp.	—	89.0 mL	
8 Tbsp. (1/2 cup)	4 fl. oz	120.0 mL	
3/4 cup	6 fl. oz	178.0 mL	
1 cup	8 fl. oz	237.0 mL	(.24 liters)
1 1/2 cups	—	354.0 mL	
1 3/4 cups	—	414.0 mL	
2 cups (1 pint)	16 fl. oz	473.0 mL	
4 cups (1 quart)	32 fl. oz	—	(.95 liters)
5 cups	—	1185.0 mL	(1.183 liters)
16 cups (1 gallon)	128 fl. oz	—	(3.8 liters)

Metric Equivalents for Butter

U.S.	Metric
2 tsp.	10.0 g
1 Tbsp.	15.0 g
1 1/2 Tbsp.	22.5 g
2 Tbsp. (1 oz)	55.0 g
3 Tbsp.	70.0 g
1/4 lb. (1 stick)	110.0 g
1/2 lb. (2 sticks)	220.0 g

Oven Temperatures

Degrees Fahrenheit	Degrees Centigrade	British Gas Marks
200°	93.0°	—
250°	120.0°	—
275°	140.0°	1
300°	150.0°	2
325°	165.0°	3
350°	175.0°	4
375°	190.0°	5
400°	200.0°	6
450°	230.0°	8

Metric Equivalents for Weight

U.S.	Metric
1 oz	28 g
2 oz	58 g
3 oz	85 g
4 oz (1/4 lb.)	113 g
5 oz	142 g
6 oz	170 g
7 oz	199 g
8 oz (1/2 lb.)	227 g
10 oz	284 g
12 oz (3/4 lb.)	340 g
14 oz	397 g
16 oz (1 lb.)	454 g

Metric Equivalents for Length
(use also for pan sizes)

U.S.	Metric
1/4 inch	.65 cm
1/2 inch	1.25 cm
1 inch	2.50 cm
2 inches	5.00 cm
3 inches	6.00 cm
4 inches	8.00 cm
5 inches	11.00 cm
6 inches	15.00 cm
7 inches	18.00 cm
8 inches	20.00 cm
9 inches	23.00 cm
12 inches	30.50 cm
15 inches	38.00 cm

Index